PROFIT FIRST

FIRST

—— *FOR* ——

COMMERCIAL
CONSTRUCTION

A BUSINESS FABLE ABOUT MASTERING
CONSTRUCTION CASH FLOW

WADE CARPENTER CPA, CGMA

FOREWORD BY **MIKE MICHALOWICZ**

Profit First for Commercial Construction
A Business Fable About Mastering Construction Cash Flow
by Wade Carpenter
Contractor Success Press
280 Country Club Dr., Ste. 100, Stockbridge, GA 30281
©2025 by Wade Carpenter

Published 2025
Printed in the United States of America

ISBN (paperback): 979-8-9929355-0-9
ISBN (ebook): 979-8-9929355-1-6
ISBN (audio): 979-8-9929355-2-3

https://profitfirstconstruction.com

Page design and typesetting by Choi Messer

DISCLAIMER: This book is for informational purposes only. Its contents should not be considered legal or financial advice. Wade Carpenter, CPA, CGMA, and Carpenter & Company, CPAs, PC, make no guarantee or other promise as to any results that may be obtained from using this content. You should do your own due diligence and consult your attorney and/or tax professional regarding questions specific to your situation.

Wade Carpenter, CPA, CGMA, and Carpenter & Company, CPAs, PC, disclaim any and all liability in the event that any information, commentary, analysis, opinions, advice, and/or recommendations herein prove to be inaccurate, incomplete, unreliable, or result in any investment or other losses.

For the contractors who weather the storms, fight the cash flow battle, and press on despite the sleepless nights—the ones who juggle payroll; pour their time, money, and sweat into something greater than themselves; and refuse to quit. The work is never easy, but your resilience builds more than structures: it builds legacy.

CONTENTS

FOREWORD

WADE DIDN'T JUST PICK ME up. He carried me. Literally.

It happened during one of our annual Profit First Professional retreats. This time we were in Arizona, where one of our activities was a behind-the-scenes tour of a local zoo. As a goof, I thought it would be funny to see if Wade and another Profit First Professional (PFP) could pick me up, carry me toward the big bear exhibit, and feign feeding me to the bear—another one of my typically silly ideas, but it seemed perfectly suited to the lighthearted mood of the day.

Now, if you know Wade, you know he's not the kind of guy whose external appearance screams, "Let's go for it!" You might not expect that someone with his calm, thoughtful demeanor would take part in a joke like this. But that's the thing about Wade. His actions speak louder than his selective words. And those actions often say, "If it serves you, hell yeah, I'm all in."

The next thing I knew, Wade and the other fella picked me up and hoisted me into the air. I'll admit, I was surprised they picked me up so easily. A little *too* easily; I quickly realized that they *could* throw me into the bear exhibit if they wanted to. Everyone else snapped photos and we all laughed.

This memory sticks with me because it perfectly encapsulates who Wade is. He's the guy who, when he sees an opportunity to help or even just be part of the fun, is all in, no matter how heavy the "lift" might be.

That mindset is exactly what makes Wade the right person to share the strategies in this book. His commitment to helping others is unparalleled, and he's proven it time and time again—not just in moments like that day at the zoo, but in his approach to his work with Profit First and the commercial construction industry.

Wade has been a Mastery-level Profit First Professional for nearly a decade. From the beginning, he didn't just adopt the system casually, but dove in headfirst, learning it, mastering it, and adapting it to the unique challenges faced by commercial contractors.

No question, construction is a tough business. Cash flow is erratic, timelines are unpredictable, and expenses can balloon overnight. Commercial contractors are masters at building physical structures, but managing their finances? That's often a different story.

Wade saw this firsthand, working with contractors who were incredible at their trade but struggling to keep their businesses afloat. Many were stuck in a cycle of feast or famine, with a few months of plentiful income followed by stretches of financial drought. Wade knew that the traditional Profit First system had the power to change that, but also that it needed to be tailored specifically to the construction industry.

And that's exactly what Wade did. He went all in, applying the same "I'll carry you" attitude to the Profit First system that he had to picking me up at the zoo. He worked tirelessly to adapt it, diving into the nuances of construction cash flow to figure out how to make the system work for contractors who operate with long project timelines and manage irregular payments. Wade made it his mission to help contractors not only stay afloat, but also truly thrive.

This book is the culmination of that work. It's a practical, fun-to-read parable designed specifically for commercial construction business owners who are tired of the financial roller coaster. In these pages, Wade breaks down the Profit First for Commercial Construction system in a way that makes sense even if you've struggled with money your entire career.

What I love about Wade's approach is that it's not just about teaching you how to handle money—it's about empowering you to take control of your business. He understands that being a contractor isn't just about building office buildings, retail spaces, and the like; it's about building a life. And you can't do that if you're constantly worried about where your next paycheck is coming from or how you're going to pay your team.

Wade walks you through each step of the Profit First for Commercial Construction system, showing you how to create financial stability no matter how unpredictable the industry may be. You'll learn how to manage cash flow in a way that prioritizes profit, ensures that you're always able to cover your expenses, and sets you up for long-term success.

But more than that, Wade is here to carry you through the process. Just like that day at the zoo when he carried me, Wade's commitment to lifting you up sets him apart. He knows the weight you carry as a commercial construction business owner; he's ready to shoulder that burden with you, and it comes to him easily.

By the time you finish reading this book, you won't just have a better grasp on your finances—you'll be permanently profitable. Every day, with every dollar, there will be money for you. And every step of the way, Wade will be your partner: someone who's gone all in on making sure you have the tools and the knowledge to run a permanently profitable business. Someone who's been in the trenches with contractors for years and knows exactly what it takes to succeed in this industry.

The work ahead may feel like a lot, but you're not doing it alone. Wade is here to guide you through the challenges, just as he's done for countless commercial contractors before you.

—Mike Michalowicz

INTRODUCTION

"Distress call from the *Kobayashi Maru,* Captain."

"Put it on speaker, Lieutenant," the captain replied.

Over the speaker came a frantic plea. "We struck a mine and lost all power. We have sustained many casualties, our hull has been breached, and our life support systems are failing. Can you assist?"

"Data on the *Kobayashi Maru*?" the captain asked.

"Eighty-one crew, three hundred passengers," the first officer replied. "Captain, they are in enemy territory."

"Plot a course for rescue, Helmsman," the captain said calmly.

"Aye, sir," the helmsman responded.

"We are now in violation of treaty, Captain," the first officer reported.

"I am aware," the captain replied.

"Captain, three enemy ships have surrounded us. They are all firing."

• • •

This is my take on a scene from a *Star Trek* movie. The *Kobayashi Maru* is a fictional training exercise designed to test a cadet's reaction to a no-win scenario, purposely planned so that there is no possible positive outcome.

Construction cash flow can seem like you live out a no-win scenario every single day.

The odds are stacked against you. You have to pay everyone else first, but your customers don't care. You are the last to eat and you are tired of being the martyr. You have no idea what your overhead truly is. You *think* you are making money on your jobs, but there never seems to be anything left over. It wasn't supposed to be this way. Why does everyone else do so much better than you? What are you doing wrong?

In *The Wrath of Khan*, Captain Kirk was famously the only cadet who "beat" the test. But he didn't win by following the rules. He reprogrammed the simulation, changing the conditions of the test so it was possible to rescue the ship.

His famous responses when asked about it were "I don't believe in a no-win scenario" and "I don't like to lose."

If you want to change the rules of your real-life game of construction cash flow, this book is for you.

Indeed, the rules of construction are stacked against you. You are expected to finance projects out of your own pocket while clients hold onto the funds, waiting until the last minute to release payment. Meanwhile, you've had to pay your people and all your overhead but haven't taken home a paycheck in weeks, sometimes months, and are behind on your own bills and taxes because of it.

But what if, like Captain Kirk, you could *rewrite the rules*? What if the system didn't have to be stacked against you?

In this book, I will teach you how to change the conditions of your own story.

This is where Profit First comes in.

Mike Michalowicz's book *Profit First* changed the rules of the game for businesses across the globe by giving owners a simple system to ensure that profit is left over, in cash, to reward them for risking entrepreneurship. Later came a derivative, *Profit First for Contractors* by Shawn Van Dyke. Both are excellent books, and Shawn's book has some great teachings about markup versus margin that contractors should know and understand. I am grateful to both authors for supporting this specialized *Profit First* derivative, and I encourage you to pick up copies of both of their books as well.

What is the difference? First, this book and the principles behind it are for all construction businesses, not just commercial contractors. I wrote it because there are so many nuances to implementing the system for construction that need to be clarified and made accessible, not just locked in a consultant's proprietary toolkit. I felt that the original system was somewhat confusing for many contractors given the intricacies of dealing with job costs, and difficult to understand and implement without better guidance.

Second, the format and approach I use in this book make it very different from other *Profit First* derivatives. I teach the Profit First concepts through the fictional story of Alex, a general contractor who struggles to navigate the narrow waters of cash flow while building a high school. His interactions with coworkers and subcontractors on the project, all also entirely fictional characters, illustrate those challenges and the Profit First concepts, applied to different types of construction, as they play out during the course of a major project.

I asked Mike Michalowicz for the rights to write this book more than five years before he agreed to approach Shawn about it. In retrospect, I see that I wasn't ready to write it until now. To be sure, I had my adaptations to the system back then, but the ensuing years have shown me a full picture of what works and what doesn't. Now, through helping many contractors implement Profit First in construction companies of all sizes, I have fully refined my approach.

In one case, I personally witnessed a contractor's total transformation. When we first met, he was hundreds of thousands of dollars in debt, owed several years' worth of back taxes, and was constantly taking out pay-by-the-week loans just to survive. Upon reaching his sixtieth birthday he had nothing saved for retirement, a business he could never take a vacation from, and was still working more than sixty-five hours a week. He didn't know what a regular paycheck was.

Now he has completely paid off his debt, including the back taxes, and hasn't missed a paycheck in the last eighteen months. He rarely works more than twenty hours a week but is maxing out his retirement savings every year. His business is healthy and has value, and he now has the option to either keep working or sell it and retire in comfort.

This didn't happen overnight, but it did happen.

I have said many times that I wish Mike had written *Profit First* before the Great Recession of 2008, which many contractors did not survive. If they had had this system in place back then, their outcomes might have been quite different.

As you read this book, you will develop that early warning system that could have saved so many. You will recognize things like the effects of seasonality on your business, what that elusive term "overhead" really means, and what happens to cash flow as you grow. You will finally have a system that enables you to sustain that growth without running out of cash. You will change your own story.

With clear examples and action steps to follow at the end of each chapter, you will learn the principles of Profit First and how to implement them in your business. Previous books on Profit First teach a seventeen-step approach to implementation. I throw that out the window and begin with simple, practical steps to help you start the system, get on top of your job costs, and chase your targets in a very different, doable way.

Why?

I want to make it easy for you to follow along and implement the steps I give you so that you change the game in your business.

Do the exercises.

Do them as you read.

Don't finish the book first.

Don't just read them and think about it.

Do them.

Captain Kirk and I will be watching.

If you don't like to lose and actually want to beat your own "no-win" cash flow scenario, read on.

PART 1

LAYING THE FOUNDATION
FOR FINANCIAL CLARITY

CHAPTER 1
Breaking Point:
A Desperate Call for Help

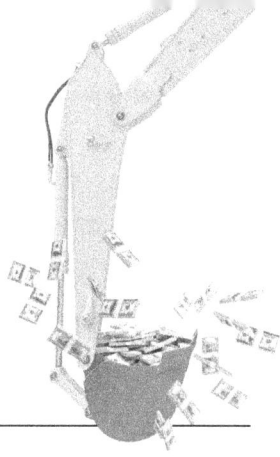

The Call That Changed Everything

ONE CHILLY, SUNNY SATURDAY MORNING, I was working on my second caffeine-laced drink of the day on my front porch when my cell phone rang at 7:30 a.m. It was Alex Turner, a contractor I hadn't heard from in three years, and he sounded desperate. He apologized for calling so early and out of the blue, but he needed help. "There's no way I can make this new school job work without bankrupting the company," he told me in a rush.

After catching his breath, he apologized profusely and asked if he had called too early. Like most of my contractor clients, I am an early riser and had been up for a couple of hours.

"No, I'm good, tell me more," I said.

I met Alex many years ago while working with a general contractor who got into cash flow trouble and didn't survive the Great Recession of 2008. Alex and I kept in touch over the years and occasionally saw each other at trade shows and construction networking events, but it had been a while since we talked.

Alex started as a laborer on a framing crew for a residential general contractor when he was a teenager. He stood out as one of those guys everybody liked and got along with—the crew and the higher-ups. As young as he was, he quickly became a team leader, managing men much older than himself. He loved learning and had a passion for figuring out how to build things and how the world works.

Alex saw how some of the older guys had worked all their lives and had little to show for it. He also noticed that the owner drove the best pickup truck and got a new one every year. Alex quickly figured out which life he wanted for himself.

A Risky Leap of Faith

WHEN WE SPOKE THAT SATURDAY morning, Alex explained that he had moved to Radcliffe & Son General Contractors as a senior project manager. RGC, as everyone called it, had transitioned from residential and multifamily construction to commercial projects in recent years. They had built a good reputation and were becoming known in construction bidding circles for various types of commercial work. Lately, they had been concentrating on school renovation jobs.

"That sounds great. Your life seems to be coming together. So what's the problem?" I asked.

"We actually got the job and now I have to build it," he said.

"What do you mean?" I asked.

Alex explained that after all the school renovation jobs, the company had finally taken the leap and bid on building a new high school from the ground up—the biggest job they had ever tackled by a long shot.

"Congratulations," I said.

"No, you don't understand. I don't have the cash flow for it." He went on to say that Dan, the boss's son, had talked his dad—Roger Radcliffe, RGC's owner—into bidding on the project. All of this had happened while Alex was away on a long hunting trip, so he knew nothing about it until he got back.

"The job is just over $19 million in revenue, which is more than double our largest job so far," Alex continued. "Dan convinced Roger that a big job was exactly what we needed to finally get out of the cash crunch we've been dealing with as we grow."

Alex told me how Dan had worked up the bid himself, while Roger had called in every favor with his bond agent that he had left to get the bid bond on the job. On paper, they estimated a $2,000,000 profit.

After Alex learned about the job, Roger asked him to review the estimate. Alex was furious because in previous discussions, they had decided RGC didn't have the resources to take on such a large project. Roger explained that they'd only had three days' notice for the bid and it was a great opportunity they couldn't pass up. In order to meet the bid deadline, Roger, Dan, and the rest of the crew had called all of Alex's favorite subcontractors, getting their bids in record time. Dan had told the subcontractors that if they ever wanted any more work from RGC, they needed to submit their estimates quickly and offer a discount, since it was a big job and RGC was doing them a favor.

Reviewing the bid, Alex quickly noticed a major miscalculation by Dan on the mechanical phase of the school build. By Alex's estimate, the bid should have been at least $1.5 million higher. Roger assured him that they had some extra padding in the contingency section to cover such issues.

A Familiar Pattern of Cash Flow Struggles

"I TOLD HIM WE'D NEED all that padding and more," Alex said to me. But Roger felt that this was their best chance to finally escape the cash flow crunch they had been facing, and Dan was convinced that if they could just reach the next level, life would become much easier.

Roger had shared a bit about the cash flow situation and Alex was in a trusted position, so he knew that every Wednesday was a constant battle to chase down payments by Thursday in order to cover payroll on Friday. Numerous phone calls, begging for wire transfers, driving a couple of hours to pick up a check—these things seemed to happen almost weekly. Alex mentioned that he had missed a few checks himself, but he was a team player and believed it would all work out in the long run. However, Alex's wife, Helen, was becoming increasingly resentful about it.

Roger told Alex that this was their chance to finally get back in the good graces of their subcontractors and materials suppliers and stop borrowing from the next job to pay for the last. But Alex was used to making deals there too—promises the company didn't always keep.

At this point, I stopped Alex and asked him if this sounded familiar. To me, it sounded like 2008 all over again. Alex had worked for Dependable Construction for most of his career and had been on the fast track to take it over from the owner, but Dependable had expanded too quickly for their cash flow, gone deeply into debt before the Great Recession, and couldn't survive the downturn.

"Exactly!" Alex said. "Déjà vu. I'm worried this could turn out the same way."

Alex told me that he, Roger, and Dan had all gone to the bid opening the day before. All the usual big players were there, including Precision Prime Contractors, RGC's archrival, a company of about the same size that always seemed to undercut other companies' bids. Alex was secretly glad to see them there and hoped they would win the job, but Roger and Dan reassured him that he shouldn't worry; they had purposely bid low enough to ensure that RGC got it. After seeing the estimate Dan had put together, Alex didn't need to ask what they meant.

The bid were opened and the county commissioner read the bids aloud one by one. RGC's bid was the second to be opened, and through the fourth bid, theirs remained the lowest by far, especially compared to a couple of the big players. That wasn't surprising because big companies always bid high. The fifth bid was Precision Prime's. To Alex's surprise, RGC's bid was still the lowest—not just low, but 9% under Precision Prime's. The rest of the bids were read and RGC was confirmed as the low bidder.

The High Cost of Winning

AS THE THREE WALKED OUT to the truck, Dan high-fived Roger but Alex didn't join in. "When I got into the truck with them, I blurted out, 'Really—9% under the lowest bid? What is the bonding company going to say? How are we going to pull this off?'"

Alex told me how Dan tried to reassure him with a "You've got this," while Roger said he had the smarts and the contacts to get it done on time and on budget—and that there would be a big bonus in it for him.

"And what did you say, Alex?" I asked.

"I didn't say anything. To be honest, all I could think was, bonus? There won't be enough cash to make this work, much less pay a bonus," Alex said. "I'd be happy just to get caught up on my missed paychecks first. The ride back to the office takes forty-five minutes, but it felt like forever because the silence was so uncomfortable."

He went on to tell me how Roger called everyone in the company into the break room to make the big announcement about the job, then told them he was taking them all to lunch to celebrate. Alex pulled Roger aside as they started out the door and said he wanted to skip the lunch because he needed to get to work right away.

I know Alex as the guy everyone gets along with, so I asked, "Was Roger OK with that?"

"I knew my absence would be noticed, but I didn't really give him a choice. To be quite frank, I didn't much care at that moment. I just jumped in my truck and left," Alex said. "Everyone knew that I didn't agree with bidding the job."

Alex explained that he was pretty much the only one capable of talking his coworkers off the ledge where Dan was involved. Dan frequently reminded everyone of his position as the boss's son and often pushed people to their breaking point. In fact, a couple of key people had left because of him, which was how Alex had been recruited. When it became clear that he didn't understand construction like Roger and Alex did, Dan had lost any remaining respect his coworkers might have had for him.

"That never stops him from joining conversations where he clearly doesn't know what he's talking about," Alex said, starting to sound a bit petty.

I stopped Alex and asked, "Does Roger not understand that Dan's lack of experience is part of the problem? Why would he allow Dan to bid the job when you disagreed with it?"

"He knows," Alex said, "but he also paid for an expensive college education for Dan. Dan got a business degree, so Roger figures he must have learned something we don't know—Roger and I have trade school educations."

"I would trade practical, on-the-job education over book education any day of the week," I said.

Alex sighed. "Roger and I have had many talks about Dan. He obviously wants his son to succeed, but also quietly admits that he has failed at just about every job he's been given at the company. He knows Dan didn't learn the ropes, but because he's trying to be a good father, he doesn't want Dan to have to go through the challenges he did."

"So where does that put you in this picture?" I asked.

"Well, it's why I was brought in and given the senior project manager title. Dan is a vice president, so even though everyone knows and trusts me, they also know Dan is ahead of me in the pecking order."

A Moment of Reckoning

ALEX CONTINUED HIS STORY. AFTER Roger reluctantly agreed to explain to the group that Alex had to skip lunch because he needed to line some things up for the job, Alex jumped in his truck and drove aimlessly down the highway, stewing over what had happened. After about thirty minutes, he found himself near the place where he had grown up. Hungry but not in the mood to talk to anyone, he stopped by a run-down little restaurant and bar he remembered from his younger years, figuring nobody would know him there. He sat in silence, eating a burger and downing three beers even though he didn't drink much, especially during the day.

He thought about how Roger expected him to be the savior and ensure that the rest of the team kept their jobs. He felt the weight on his shoulders from knowing he was the one who had to make sure that his subcontractors, many of whom were great friends, got paid. He reflected on the relationships he had built with materials suppliers over the years—they would be counting on him to pull this off and get them paid too. He worried about the 10% retainage clause that would stretch RGC's cash flow to the breaking point by the project's end. Alex's phone kept ringing, but he silenced it and stopped looking at the caller ID.

He sat there for two and a half hours, long after the lunch crowd was gone and the waitress had cleared his plate. She kept coming over to see if he needed anything else, but eventually she told him that they closed after lunch, apologized, and asked him to pay his bill.

The effects of three beers had worn off, but Alex didn't want to go too far. He jumped in his truck and drove about half a mile down the road. He passed his old high school, which had been shut down years earlier. He laughed when he noticed that the letters *C* and *L* had fallen off the sign and it was now a "HIGH SHOO."

He thought about how the red brick shell of the building was still there, but the soul of the place was gone. It was built so long ago—how solid its foundation must be. Those good bones were all that held the place up now.

It was a shame that it was starting to crumble. The grass was overgrown and nobody went there anymore.

Alex drove his truck up the pothole-filled service road to the top of the hill where he and his friends used to park as teenagers, pulled under a tree, and looked down at the town where he had grown up. From this vantage point, he could see several miles around the valley. He glanced over at the industrial area and saw the building where he had worked his first construction job. He remembered going there after school and learning the ropes. That company was long gone now, and the dingy blue metal building's roof was rusted. He saw several broken windows.

Even back then, he recalled, there were weeks when his paycheck was late. At the time, he didn't understand why—but on that job, he started to notice that the owner always drove a shiny new pickup truck and seemed to have it made. Everyone in business management drove nice pickup trucks, so Alex thought construction must be a gold mine to be tapped. He remembered not being able to work in the winter and times when the company didn't have any work for him, but he figured the boss never missed a meal.

As he sat there, Alex realized that he'd forgotten how far he had come. He thought about the fact that he was making a lot more money now and had more respect from the higher-ups. He drove a nice pickup now, courtesy of RGC. He didn't have to worry about getting laid off in the winter or not making money when the company had no work. He thought about how he had a wife and two wonderful kids he wished he had more time with. The problems were different now: dealing with suppliers and subcontractors, coordinating schedules, and trying to keep up and control the chaos. Everyone was counting on him.

Alex told me that at that moment, sitting in his truck, he wished he still had that simpler life—a life of loving construction, learning to build, and figuring things out. He missed computing compound angles on crown molding and watching a rough frame take shape as something beautiful he was proud of. He missed the ease and freedom of his earlier life, when he didn't have so many people depending on him. Meanwhile, his phone kept ringing, and the text messages kept coming.

"Then I got a call from Helen," Alex said.

"Uh-oh! Were you in trouble?" I asked.

"Not with her. I got the 'Oh, thank God! Are you OK? Everyone is looking for you. I thought you might have been in an accident. Your office called and they haven't seen you since this morning.' I told her I was fine, just clearing my head, and let her know we got the job."

"Did she know how you felt?" I asked.

"She's heard me talk about it for weeks. She also told me she knew about winning the bid—I guess Roger couldn't wait to tell her when he called looking for me. We talked about being pissed off at Dan again and then she asked when I was coming home." He paused. "I had no idea it was after four o'clock. I couldn't believe I had been sitting up there for almost two hours."

Alex realized that he had better check in at work, but he didn't want to talk to anybody. He decided to text Pam back, figuring that she wouldn't give him the third degree, and let her know he wouldn't be back at the office that day.

"Who's Pam?" I asked.

I learned that Pam Fields was RGC's office manager and Roger's assistant. She had been at RGC for about six months, having worked for other contractors, and boasted a strong construction bookkeeping background—on her résumé, at least. Alex liked Pam and said that she seemed knowledgeable. Like him, she had been brought in to hopefully help change RGC's path, in particular their accounting system—again.

Alex went on to tell me that she was the second bookkeeper they'd hired in the last year and had been promising job cost reports that never seemed to materialize. Now, six months since she started, Alex never got reports on time, and when they did show up, they didn't make sense. He didn't trust the numbers.

Pam was also tasked with implementing new software that Dan had impulsively bought two years before at a trade show. The software cost them several thousand dollars a month and they were no closer to implementing it than when they first bought it. Alex had spent countless hours with Pam trying to improve the accounting system, but it seemed like they were no further along than when they started.

"That's pretty common," I reassured him.

"I know, but it gets worse," Alex said.

Alex told me how accounting was a touchy subject at RGC. Roger's first wife, was a schoolteacher who did RGC's books on the side, but was never trained in accounting and hated it. After years of Roger never bringing home a consistent paycheck and never spending time with the family because he worked constantly, and always having to cover the company taxes with her teaching paycheck, she had come to resent Roger.

Then there was the "incident." Without telling her, Roger had wiped out their savings and maxed out her personal credit card to cover the cash flow for a job.

"The result was a particularly nasty divorce," Alex said.

"That definitely happens—more often than you might think," I offered.

"I bet, but she became the reason everything was the way it was."

He told me that after the divorce, Roger blamed all the headaches on his ex-wife, claiming that her inability to keep up with accounting or provide good job cost records was the reason for their cash flow problems. RGC had gone through a string of bookkeepers since then, none lasting more than a year. Now it was Pam's turn.

"What did Pam say when you texted back?" I asked.

"She told me that Roger was pissed and wanted to know where I had been. I figured I had better have some excuse, so I told her I was talking to contractors about the job," Alex said.

"Does Pam understand the problem with cash flow, with this kind of growth?" I asked.

"Pam said everything would be all right when the profits show up," Alex replied. "Do you think she gets it?"

"No, it doesn't seem she gets the cash flow issues," I said. "Everyone always thinks more sales is the cure."

"Yep," Alex said. "Anyway, I just told her to tell Roger I would be back on Monday. I guess at that moment, I didn't care what he thought. I just cranked up my truck and headed for home after that."

A Meeting That Could Change Everything

As Alex finished relaying his story, he admitted that he hadn't slept much that night. Not knowing how Dan played into things, he had left a really good job based on Roger's promises. Now he wondered if any of those promises were genuine and realized that he had staked his career on moving to RGC. Knowing I had helped several contractors with their accounting and cash flow, he asked if the two of us could set up a meeting with Roger.

"I don't think he sees the problems I see with this job," Alex said.

"I suspect Roger may understand more than you think about how critical this is," I replied. "Of course, set it up. I'd be glad to meet him."

Alex called back about three hours later.

"I had a good talk with Roger," he said, "and he confided in me that he was a bit worried too, especially after hearing our bid was so much lower than Precision Prime's. He asked me to keep this meeting from Dan."

We set up a late morning meeting at their office for the following Wednesday.

//

CHAPTER 1 END NOTES
Change the Conditions of the Test

The struggles Alex faced occur every day in the construction world. Everyone has their hand out and the money can't come in fast enough, much less leave any for you to take care of yourself. Right now, this may seem overwhelming and unfixable. You may be asking yourself if you should have stuck it out working for someone else. Trust me, it does get better—in fact, construction can be quite lucrative. You just need to learn to control your cash flow.

Stick with me, do the work, and follow the steps I give you, and by the time you finish reading this book, your life will have begun to change for the better. I'm not telling you it will happen overnight, but a new path will emerge.

Imagine trying to turn a large, rusted flywheel that hasn't moved in years. At first, it feels like your effort barely makes a difference. It may take all of your strength to move the wheel just an inch. But as you keep pushing, the rust slowly breaks away and, little by little, the wheel begins to turn. Every turn becomes a bit easier, and with every push, the wheel gains more speed. Eventually, your steady effort builds so much momentum that the flywheel turns on its own and requires far less energy to keep it going.

It's going to be like that.

For now, remember that success builds upon success—and it does get easier.

Commit to me, and yourself, that you will do the exercises I've created for you. They are all doable without a fancy advanced degree. I will explain what to do and how to turn around your profitability even if your books are in poor shape now. You don't have to finish the book first to start making changes.

In fact, I don't want you to.

Do the exercises at the end of each chapter as you follow along with the story. You may feel that some of the sections and ideas don't apply to you—read them anyway. Don't try to shortcut the process.

You can do this, and I want you to be held accountable as you start turning your own flywheel.

The homework for this first chapter is about as simple as it gets.

First, go to https://profitfirstconstruction.com/resources and download the figures and exercises to follow along in the book.

Second, send me an email at wade@profitfirstconstruction.com with "I don't like to lose!" in the subject line. Put "I am changing my cash flow game!" in the body of the email. Beyond that, feel free to tell me anything you like about why you are doing this.

I am rooting for you, and just know, I will read every single email.

It's time to take your first step toward a different life for yourself.

CHAPTER 2
Facing Reality:
Cash Confrontations

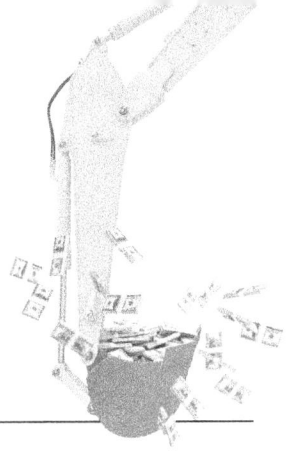

A Tense Arrival

As I DROVE INTO RGC's gravel parking lot for our meeting, I noticed a nearly new-looking RGC sign proudly displayed on the faded gray steel and brick building and looked up to see Alex's husky frame already walking toward my truck. His thick brown beard was as neatly trimmed as ever, but the worry on his face was unmistakable. As I stepped out, he said, "I've got to talk to you before we meet with Roger."

"OK," I said as we shook hands. "What's up?"

"Remember, Roger told me to keep this meeting from Dan. If he asks, just tell him you're an auditor for the bonding company or something. Roger's a bit pissed at Dan right now. Also, a warning, he's feeling unsure about what you could possibly do to help."

I agreed, wondering what that was all about.

As we walked in, Alex introduced me to Pam, the bookkeeper. I guessed that Pam was in about her mid-forties. She had nice jet-black hair with streaks of gray she wasn't hiding.

"Very nice to meet you," Pam said. "I've been looking forward to this meeting." She offered to grab drinks for us as she rushed me straight into the conference room.

Roger was already seated at the head of the table, reviewing some papers. He glanced up and then stood as we were introduced. Roger was a big guy, gray-haired and balding with a full black and gray beard. He had obviously been in this game for a while; the permanent bags under his eyes suggested years of losing sleep over the hassles of running a construction business and dealing with cash flow worries.

Pam handed around waters when all four of us were seated around the table. There was a brief moment of polite silence, the kind that felt like the calm before the storm—a quiet intensity hanging in the air that made it clear this wasn't just a casual check-in.

Skepticism About Profit First

"Alex told me about you and that you brought up the book *Profit First*. I've heard of it and even tried it, but there's no way it can deal with what contractors have to go through with cash flow," Roger said, a little defensively. "I get the concept, but I know how my business is doing by what's in my bank account."

"OK, but do you really know how you're doing?" I asked.

That's when an uncontrolled grunt or laugh—I'm not sure which—came from Pam, who was sitting across from me. "Sorry," she apologized to Roger.

"Well, we've been working on the job costing system, that's what Pam is laughing about," Roger said. "But I have a gut feel for how my jobs are doing by what's in my bank account and I know my jobs."

"You probably do have a gut feel for your jobs or can do back-of-the-napkin calculations," I said. "To address your comment about Profit First, it completely changed my firm's profitability and cash flow, and I have helped many contractors turn their situation around once they realize the habits we all have around money. The first step is to recognize them—then we can change our cash flow game. We don't do this by changing the innate behaviors, but by keeping them in mind as we implement the system. We will come back to that, but let's stick with job costing for now. Often, when we really dive into it, contractors are surprised to find that the jobs they think are making money may actually be killing their companies."

"Really?" Roger said. "I never really understood what's involved in job costing and overhead. That's the kind of work the auditors do when they create financial statements—they always tank my jobs. Anyway, Alex did mention the conversation you had with him about splitting out your money with a purpose. We have one main bank account and, oh yeah, a savings account, but that's all we need."

"I thought you said you tried Profit First and it didn't work. Did you set up the bank accounts?" I asked.

"Well, I set up an account to buy a building and threw money in there when I had extra, say if money came in from retainage and we didn't need to spend it right then," Roger explained. "That's actually the savings account."

"That's not really Profit First," I said. "I thought you said you read the book?"

"Well, I read the first couple of chapters," Roger said. "I got the concept, but then he started talking about terms I didn't understand, like 'Instant Assessments' and 'Real Revenue,' and I didn't know what to do. I also thought my banker would laugh me out of the bank for adding all those accounts, so that's the way I did it."

"So what happened?" I asked.

"Well, we had a big workers' comp audit hit unexpectedly," Roger said, "and I blew an engine in my truck at the same time. I had to use the money."

"How much is in the account now?" I asked.

"About a hundred dollars," Pam said. "We keep enough in there to cover the service charges."

The Cash Flow Rollercoaster

"IN CONSTRUCTION, MONEY COMES IN and usually disappears just as fast," I said. "A lot of money comes in and you feel like you're on top of the world. Then the next day, it disappears, and you feel like the world is coming to an end."

As soon as I said that, Roger, Alex, and Pam all started talking at the same time, then abruptly stopped. It was obvious that they understood what I was getting at. They looked at each other in silence for a moment, and I purposely let them stew.

Then Roger blurted out, "OK, I guess I didn't do it right and never finished the book. I'm not much of a reader. But the part I did get to implied that job costs don't matter and that I wasn't a two-million-dollar contractor, which is where I was at the time. That's a load of crap. I was proud to get to that two-million-dollar a year revenue mark. I worked my butt off to get there."

"No doubt you did," I said. "Construction is a tough business. If you look at the statistics, the odds of any business making it to even the one-million-dollar mark are low, and the odds of surviving past the first five years are even lower. Unfortunately, the survival rates of contractors are even worse. Poor cash flow and financial management are major causes."

"We know," Pam said.

Alex chimed in, "Roger shared more with me after we spoke the other day. It doesn't look good for us. The bank is concerned, and the bonding company is really nervous, but they're on the hook now. They gave us the bid bond for the high school job before we finished our financials for the year. I called in every favor I had left with them, and they will be watching us like a hawk."

"So what didn't you get about the concept?" I asked. "Allocating money really is key to implementing Profit First."

"Well, I didn't have good books then and with all the new terms, I really didn't know what to do," Roger said, looking at Pam. "I may not have great job costing now, but hopefully I have things in the right buckets, at least."

The Reality of RGC's Numbers

"WE'LL COME BACK TO THAT," I assured Roger. Then I turned to Pam and asked, "What is the gross margin the company is making on jobs?"

She looked at me, not really understanding what I was asking. Roger said, "We make at least 40% on all of our jobs."

"No, it's more like a 20% gross margin at best before overhead," Alex corrected.

"Do you have a profit and loss statement?" I asked.

"Yes," Pam said. "Let me go get it." She started to rise.

"Can you give me the last five years of profit and loss statements?" I asked.

"We only have a couple of years in the system," Pam said.

"How about tax returns?" I asked.

"Pam, go get the tax returns out of the files and bring them in here," Roger said.

As Pam left the room, Alex and Roger looked at each other for a moment. Then Alex muttered, "She can get the financials, but we don't trust the numbers."

"We do our best to keep up," Roger said. "We used that online soft-ware everyone uses for several years. The numbers fed right in from the banks and credit cards, and it was supposed to be easy and built for contractors, but it never worked. Then we tried a couple of software apps that were supposed to make job costing super simple. They cost us a big monthly subscription for a few years."

"So they didn't work either?" I asked, though I already knew the answer.

"No," Roger said. "After three years of paying for the add-on software and three years of having my CPA clean it up, we finally gave up on it. They already charged an arm and a leg to fix it every year, but after adding the job costing software, it went through the roof. We never got good job cost numbers."

"So where are you now?" I asked.

"Well, about two years ago, I sent Dan to a trade show," Roger explained. "He came back and talked me into buying what the sales rep told him was the end-all-be-all software for construction contractors. It was supposed to cost about twenty thousand dollars, but we are way past that now. They added a lot more for features we supposedly needed. Then there's the cost of the consultants, which has now dwarfed the cost of the software, and I still don't know where we are. Pam at least sort of knew her way around the online software, but now we're late filing our taxes for last year because the CPA is having a bigger problem than ever cleaning it up. We sent an in-house financial statement to the bonding company, and that's when everything really started to unravel."

Roger looked harried. As he took a breath, I chimed in, "Well, there is a simpler way of looking at this that I think you need to consider right now to get on top of your cash flow."

Dan Joins the Meeting

AT THIS POINT, PAM CAME back with a bunch of loose papers and folders. She was followed by Dan, who had apparently been listening outside the conference room's closed door.

"I didn't know we were meeting," Dan said, stepping forward to introduce himself with an outstretched hand. I couldn't help but notice his crisp new button-down shirt; it looked more suited to a finance intern than someone who belonged on a construction site. He had his father's sharp facial features, but none of his presence—his frame was wiry, almost underfed, and his handshake was the kind that tried too hard for firmness. His neatly combed hair and carefully polished shoes contrasted starkly with Alex's work boots and calloused hands.

"I'm Dan, Vice President of Operations," he said boastfully, "and I'm glad to help. Nice to meet you, and you are…?"

I glanced at Alex and said, "Hi, I'm Wade. I'm a consultant for the bonding company."

Roger said, "Dan, we've got this."

"No, I want to help," Dan said, obviously determined to stay in the room.

Pam handed me several printouts and the tax returns. I said, "OK, Dan, how much do you make on your jobs? What's your gross margin?"

"We always make 35% on our jobs," Dan said confidently.

I started to examine the balance sheet Pam had given me and immediately noticed things that looked out of place, like receivables with a balance that couldn't possibly be right and had been growing for a number of years. I saw over- and under-billing amounts that hadn't been adjusted in years. There were credit cards with negative balances and an undeposited funds account with well over a million dollars in it that had been building year after year. Then I looked at the profit and loss statement and saw negative numbers in the cost of sales that didn't make sense, misclassified loans, and several other things that instantly threw up red flags for me. After all my years working with contractors, I knew that I couldn't trust these numbers either.

"Let me look at the tax returns," I said.

I knew the firm that had prepared them—a good local CPA firm that did fair work but took every company in any industry that could pay them. It was obvious that they had done some work to reconcile the numbers outside of the company books, but even though there were some numbers that I questioned on the returns, I figured that for purposes of my calculations today they would be good enough and reasonably in the ballpark. I quickly scribbled some numbers from each of the last five years on my notepad.

Introducing the JobEx Concept

As I DID THIS, I said, "These tax returns are on a cash basis, which is good for what we need today. Even if a contractor has no books, I can get a snapshot of where they are by doing an analysis of what I call 'JobEx.' It is short for 'job expenses,' and it is my surrogate gut-check on your job costing and how it is affecting your cash flow."

"Another term like 'Real Revenue' or that 'Instant Assessment' thing I didn't understand?" Roger asked.

"We will get to all of that, but this is simpler," I said. "I actually don't recommend that contractors start with the Instant Assessment. It's a distraction and why I start differently. I have adapted the process to give contractors a first pass at whether they are bidding properly. You see, the original *Profit First* was written for all audiences, not just contractors, and no book since has really explained the nuances of construction Real Revenue and how to apply it."

"There's that term again, 'Real Revenue,'" Alex said.

"Yes, Mike Michalowicz came up with a pretty clear definition of it that is brilliant in its simplicity," I said, continuing to scribble numbers from the tax return onto my notepad. "It is just a matter of adding up materials and subcontractors and then subtracting that from the total revenue. It doesn't go far enough in construction, but let's stick with that basic definition for a minute."

"Just our materials and subcontractor costs?" Pam asked.

"Yes," I said. "Assuming Roger is doing the two million in revenue he mentioned a while ago, let's use that as an example."

"We are much more than that now," Dan said proudly. "I thought you said you were with the bonding company. What does any of this have to do with a bond?"

"For easy math, let's stick with two million now," I said, ignoring his question about who I was with. "If you make 30% gross profit on your jobs, the other 70% probably isn't just materials and subcontractors, but let's start with that."

"Since we subcontract most of our projects out, that's fair," Alex said. "We did start doing some of this in-house to pick up the margin on the jobs and not give it away to the subcontractors, but that really is only a fraction of the job."

Revenue vs. Reality

"I UNDERSTAND," I CONTINUED. "MY point is that right now we don't know what that true number is, and you don't have a handle on the job costs. Humor me and let's just say you make 30% as you previously stated on your jobs. Let's also assume all of the costs are materials and subs. That means your costs are 70% of the total revenue, right?"

"Right," said Alex. "Understood."

"So if we're calling you a two-million-dollar contractor and 70% goes out to materials and subs, then you are really a six-hundred-thousand-dollar contractor."

"This is stupid. We are way more than that," Dan said, obviously offended. "And do you mean to tell me that the bank and the bonding company that supposedly sent you don't think we are a big deal? That the accountants who reviewed our financial statements were wrong? You mean to tell me all those costs mean nothing?"

"Nobody doubts what revenue you have, or that you have those costs," I said. "I have worked with contractors over the last thirty-five years as an auditor, a tax accountant, and a CFO. As a CPA, I have to live with cost principles that are different from generally accepted accounting principles and the IRS. That's not the point."

"What *is* the point?" Dan asked loudly. "And what do you mean by different cost principles?"

"DAN!" Roger said even louder, in that tone a father uses when he wants his kid to shut up. "Wade, please continue."

At that moment, I felt bad for Dan—a grown man being called out in front of everybody by his dad—so I tried to smooth it over. "It's OK, Dan, we will get to the confusion about what job cost is, but let's get this principle down now: If 70% of the revenue that comes in has to go out in materials and subcontractors, that isn't your money."

"What do you mean it isn't my money?" Roger asked.

"That money has to go out to other people; it isn't your money," I said.

"What about overhead?" Alex asked.

"Overhead is something else we need to tackle, but for now, I want you to understand that when money comes in, you need to put the money that goes out to other people in a separate account. That way, when you need it to pay for those materials and subcontractors, it is there. This is a critical first step in getting you out of the 'borrow from the next job to pay for the last job' situation that you are in."

"Construction isn't that simple, and you don't understand," Dan said smugly, folding his arms and sitting back in his chair.

"It is that simple," I said. "You can only live off what is left over after you've set aside the money that goes out to other people, so let's test that on your numbers. After looking at the numbers Pam brought me, I think you are fooling yourselves."

"How so?" Roger asked.

"This is my time-tested technique I use with contractors," I said. "If a contractor has paid their subcontractors anything, at the end of each year, they have to provide them with 1099 forms for their taxes. Even if a contractor has no books, they can just add up the payments they recorded in their check register.

"It's the same thing with materials suppliers and subcontractors—we can usually just go to vendor bills, credit card statements, and checks to add up the numbers. I've had a few clients get reports from their supply houses. Once you have that total, you simply divide that number by the revenue for the year to get your percentage."

"OK, so what did you find in the tax returns?" Pam asked.

"What do you think the number was?" I asked. "Ignore what you think 'job costs' are supposed to be. Just write down what you think materials and subcontractor expenses represent as a percentage of RGC's total income. Write it on a piece of paper and hand it to me. Don't show it to anybody else."

They passed me their slips of paper and I read out the results: "Alex said 80%. Pam has 75%, Dan says 55%, and Roger has 70% for materials and subs."

"Who is right?" Pam asked.

"None of you," I said. "When I added up those categories just now and divided the total by the revenue, your best year showed that they were actually over 90% of the total revenue."

"No way," Dan said.

I flipped my notepad around to show them that over the last five years, 90% or more of the revenues that came in were in fact represented by materials and subcontractors. "In some years, they were actually greater than 100% compared to revenue," I said.

"Well, those were some bad years," Roger shot back.

"I know—they were for many contractors. As we came out of the COVID-19 pandemic, the cost of lumber and supplies, material prices all across the board went through the roof. Many people got stuck with fixed-price contracts. I completely understand that those years may have been the exception. I also understand that many times, contractors skew the numbers by holding off on collections, paying all their bills at the end of the year, or dating checks before the end of the year to avoid paying taxes."

"That's what a good CPA does, right?" Roger said.

"I get it," I said. "I haven't met a contractor yet who likes paying taxes, and I understand the deferral games. You can manipulate the numbers sometimes, but there are only so many deferral games you can play over a five-year period, and these materials and subs have consistently not been 70% or 55% as you suggested. The best year was 90% of revenue."

"So what does that mean?" Alex asked. "How can we use this?"

"Well, again, this number can be skewed," I said, "but over a five-year period, that is hard to sustain, and patterns develop. It is usually one of two things: either you have been in growth mode and cash flow has outpaced revenue, or—the most likely scenario—you don't know your numbers to bid properly."

At that moment, Alex, Pam, and Roger all looked at Dan. Later, I realized that I had accidentally stepped in something when I found out he was infamous for estimating jobs that lost money. People were angry with him; nobody had gotten bonuses last year since two of his jobs tanked badly, leaving the company strapped for cash.

Now Roger had trusted Dan with the bid on this high school project, and after Alex reviewed it, they all knew they were in trouble. On top of that, I later learned that Dan had gone out and bought a new truck for himself right after winning the bid on the school job to celebrate. They didn't even have the contract signed yet, much less the first mobilization draw, and he had already spent money he didn't have.

"Anyway, the first thing I would do is open a new bank account for these expenses," I said. "Give it a name—I call it 'JobEx.' Then, for every dollar that comes in, carve out the appropriate percentage and deposit it in that account. Only pay for your materials and subcontractors from that account.

"Again, 'JobEx' is my term for job expenses. This isn't true job costing, so I don't call the account 'Job Cost.' It's not the same thing. In construction, expenses may include more than materials and subs, so

I have adapted the definition some for the construction industry. We will come back to that, but what you need to remember is that we are talking about carving out the cash from a job that goes to other people."

"Well, since nobody knows what job cost is supposed to be anyway, I think it's a made-up number," Roger said. "I tell all of my estimators that they should put everything in the job cost number, sometimes literally including the kitchen sink. If they did that and included it in their bids, we would never lose money on a job."

"Yeah, but it isn't fair for my jobs to get hit with depreciation expenses on the trucks, or the workers' comp insurance or payroll taxes," Dan said. "I shouldn't bear the repair and maintenance costs on the company equipment. It is just Dad's way of making sure he doesn't have to pay out bonuses."

"That's precisely the point *Profit First* makes with just using materials and subs. The author's goal was to simplify the definition of what you have left over, and he did it beautifully. As a CPA and auditor, I must follow generally accepted accounting principles in the US when I do a financial statement. If companies do business internationally, they generally have to follow a separate set of rules that fall under international accounting standards. When you do a tax return, depending on the type of construction and the amount of revenue, there can be different rules for what goes into job cost. They aren't consistent, even when it comes to the IRS."

"I didn't know that," Pam said.

"As Roger mentioned, management often wants to put everything in there to cover the job costs," I said. "I see other extremes, where internal books only show the direct costs and don't try to add in any of the indirect costs. The key is to be consistent when tracking it, and you really do need to get your job cost straightened out. Right now, it is even more important that you have a clear, simple definition of it for the purpose of controlling cash flow, and from what I am hearing and seeing, you need to get on top of that pretty fast."

"Gross profit or not, we're going to make it up on the volume of the school job," Dan said. "All our overhead will be covered. You will see, and you will thank me for saving this company." He got up and stormed out of the room.

Not knowing what to say, I blurted, "I'm sorry, I didn't mean to—"

Roger cut me off. "It isn't you or anything you said." He blew out a deep breath. "Alex and Pam, do you mind leaving us for a few minutes?"

"Of course," Alex said, and Pam nodded. They left the room quietly, closing the door behind them.

"Wade, Dan doesn't understand." Roger said. "I have kept him in the dark about a lot of this. He hasn't sweated through late nights getting the billing out the door or had to get up before sunrise to get to a job. I put in years of doing hard work on the jobsite all day and then doing paperwork all night, scrambling to get bids out the door, and chasing money to cover payroll. We have kept all our people paid—well, except me, so that hopefully, my son could have an easier and better life. I keep thinking that one day this will all pay off, but I'm not getting any younger."

"You haven't been getting paid?" I asked. "Alex said he had missed some paychecks too."

"Yeah, I'm even more embarrassed about that," Roger said. "He knew we were having trouble getting money in and offered to wait on his check one week. It has been a constant problem, though, and after the first time, it was easier to ask. Now his wife is pissed at him and, I guess, me because of it. Dan hasn't missed any checks though, so don't mention any of this to Alex. I really need his expertise to pull off this job and I can't afford to lose him. How is it that everybody else is doing so much better than me?"

The Illusion of Contractor Success

"You would be surprised by how many other contractors have the same problems," I said. "Everyone always thinks the grass is greener. Nobody wants to admit when things aren't going well or how cash flow is kicking their ass in this business."

"But everybody always says how well they're doing at the trade shows, and they show up in new trucks every year," Roger said. "Several of my friends in this business have very nice offices. As I struggled to get this company off the ground, I kept telling myself, if I can just get to a half million in revenue, everything will change. Then it was, OK, I just need to get to a million and it will all get better. Then it was two million, and last year, I was approaching ten million in revenue. All I've done is get deeper in debt and introduce new problems at every level."

"That's more common than you might imagine," I said.

"This is supposed to be my retirement, but I don't see how I could stop," Roger said in a depressed tone.

"I saw some of your subcontractors' vehicles in the parking lot," I said. "They also have some nice new trucks. Does that really mean that they are doing better than you?"

"I guess not," Roger said. "Heck, I thought Precision was doing so well, but since we got the high school job instead of them, I had a couple of their guys contact me to see if I had any openings. Sounds like there are cash flow issues with them too. I always thought they were so much bigger and better run."

The "Bigger Boat" Fallacy

"DID YOU EVER SEE THE movie *Jaws*?" I asked.

Roger nodded yes.

"Remember the scene where Roy Scheider says, 'We're going to need a bigger boat'? Everybody thinks they need a bigger boat or, to put it differently, just a little more revenue and they will be over the hump. Unfortunately, what usually happens is that they find themselves deeper in debt and saddled with more overhead. That is the natural progression unless you take control of it. I just want you to know that there is a simple way to do that. Right now, you need to change your game. In fact, you need to change the rules."

"It just makes no sense that I can't take a regular paycheck," Roger said. "My wife—Dan's stepmother—doesn't even know we're still paying taxes from three years ago. It seems like I'm running a company for the benefit of my employees, for the subs, for all of the materials suppliers—everybody but me."

"That's why we need to start putting the money into different buckets—so you're able to pay yourself a decent wage and pay your taxes," I said. "We also need to make sure you have some profit left over to reward yourself for taking the risk of being in business."

"Profit," Roger snorted. "What does that mean, anyway? My CPA tells me that I have profit to pay taxes on, but it isn't in my bank account, so where is it? I asked him if it was in his account, because it sure wasn't in mine. He sat there and looked at me as if I was crazy, but he didn't have an answer."

"You know when the flight attendant comes on the loudspeaker before the flight takes off and does the safety drill?" I asked. "You know, if the plane loses pressure, you need to put your mask on before you help others."

"That's a great concept," Roger said, putting his hand up. "I've heard that before, but so many people depend on me."

"I understand, but if you can't learn to run the company so that it at least covers your salary and taxes—much less any profit—who else will if you can't work any longer?" I asked.

"Well, I was hoping Dan," Roger said. "I always thought he could take it over and turn things around. Unfortunately, he doesn't have the work ethic that I do or that Alex does."

"Exactly, so who else will do all that you do without getting paid?" I asked. "Alex won't do it forever, especially if you don't make some serious changes."

"Nobody in their right mind would," Roger said.

"So you have to learn to run the company to help yourself first. Then you can help everyone else," I replied.

Meeting to Chart a New Path

"Amen to that!" Roger said. He had brightened a little. "I'm still skeptical, but can you help us? I have to drive to a jobsite now, but could we meet again soon?"

"Sure, can we meet for lunch?" I asked.

"That would be great," Roger said. "Could I bring Alex?"

"Sure," I replied.

"One condition. You don't tell Dan," Roger said.

"No problem," I said.

"Where do you want to go?" Roger asked. "I will buy you the best steak or whatever you want."

"I know just the place," I said. "There is something you both need to see."

///

CHAPTER 2 END NOTES
Job Expenses from a Cash Perspective

WHEN NEW CONTRACTOR CLIENTS COME to see me, an almost universal complaint is that they need better cost information so they can manage their jobs better. They need information that they trust is accurate, and it must be timely, or it is of little use. They want to know that a job is going off track as soon as possible so they have time to do something about it. In an ideal world, I want you to ultimately achieve a great awareness of how you are truly doing on your jobs.

If you don't have perfect job cost records yet, or even if you never achieve anything close, for that matter, that's OK—we don't need them to fix your cash flow problems.

As you learned in this chapter, the term "job cost" can mean different things to different people, whether in formal financial statements for your banker or bonding company or when you report to the IRS. It can mean something different internally in our companies, too, such as the project manager who aims for a job profitability bonus versus the owner who wants to make sure all the costs are covered.

The lesson here is that we need a common definition of job cost that we can all agree on for the purposes of managing our cash. We'll expand on this later, but for now, forget whatever preconceived notions you have about what "job cost" is, stick with me, and let's define it as the original *Profit First* book did—as, simply, materials and subcontractors. So that we are clear on our terms, I'm going to call it "JobEx" (short for "job expenses").

Here's what I want you to do:

Step 1. First, before looking at any spreadsheets, profit and loss statements, or whatever you have, write down what you think you spend on materials and subcontractors as a percentage of the revenue you bring in. Go on, get a pen and piece of paper and write it down. Don't keep reading yet, just write down the percentage. Once you've done that, put that piece of paper aside and don't look at it.

Step 2. Next, I want you to go find out what that percentage really is. If you have profit and loss statements, gather them for the last five years. Write down the percentages for each of the last five years.

    a. Don't have profit and loss statements, but do have tax returns? That will do. Pull the numbers off of them.

    b. Don't have tax returns or profit and loss statements? That's OK— go pull your bank statements for the last twelve months and add up the figures. If you issued 1099 forms to your subcontractors, total those too.

    c. Don't have your materials total? Go through your materials bills for the last twelve months and add them up. You can also ask your supply house to give you a statement for last year.

You also need the revenue you earned from the same twelve-month period, or preferably the last five years if you have the data.

Whatever you come up with may not be perfect—that's OK. Just do it.

Lost? See Figure 2 below for an example.

The key is to take your best stab at the numbers and not skip this. Once you have the numbers, write down the percentage that your JobEx represents for each of the year(s) you reviewed. Don't move on until you have done this.

Step 3. The last step is to pick up that piece of paper from Step 1 and compare what you thought your JobEx percentage was with what you calculated in Step 2.

Were you close? Does the difference surprise you?

Keep these numbers, because we will use and refine them as we move forward.

Let's get to it!

Figure 2. Preliminary Assessment of JobEx Percentage

Step 1. Preliminary Estimate:

JobEx as a Percentage of Revenue	_____ %

Step 2. Your Actual Numbers:

	Example	Your Numbers
Revenue	$ 1,000,000	$ _____
Materials	200,000	
Subcontractors	350,000	_____
Total Job Expenses	$ 550,000	$ _____
Job Expenses as a Percentage of Revenue	55%	_____ %

CHAPTER 3

Lunch with Lessons: Understanding Cash Flow Essentials

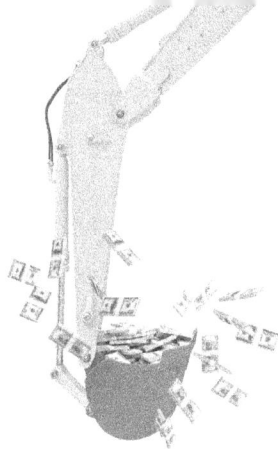

Megan's Buffet

ALEX, ROGER, AND I SET up a meeting for the following Wednesday. I asked them to meet me for an early lunch at a small buffet restaurant in an aging strip mall. I wanted to beat the lunch crowd and show them a few things. I arrived a few minutes early, and Alex and Roger were already in the entryway waiting for me.

"Lunch is on me," Alex said as we greeted each other. "I can take you to a nicer place if you want. You're doing me a favor, and I appreciate you meeting with us."

"Thanks, but Roger already tried," I said. "I really like this place and had a specific reason for choosing it."

The buffet wasn't a chain; it had good food and was spotlessly clean. As we walked in, we were immediately welcomed by the owner, Megan Scott, with whom I'd become friends after several months of enjoying her food.

We paid for the buffet and found a table in the corner. Almost as soon as we sat down, Roger told me he had something to get off his chest. He had already told me more about RGC's dire cash flow situation over the phone—now he told me the story of Dan driving up in a shiny new pickup truck the Monday after the bid opening.

I looked at Alex, wondering what I could or couldn't say.

Alex spoke up. "It's OK. Roger and I already had a long talk, and he filled me in on the situation. RGC has caught up with a few weeks of my back pay too—but now I understand better what dire straits the company is in."

"Dan has been put on a short leash," Roger added.

"Spending money you don't have is pretty common. People are naturally wired to behave in certain ways with money but are mostly unconscious of doing it," I said. "I promise that, by the end of this lunch, you will have a better understanding of this."

"OK, have at it," said Alex.

"Let me tell you a bit about Megan, the owner of this restaurant. She gets up at the crack of dawn every day to prepare food for the lunch and dinner crowds. She's constantly cleaning, cooking, serving, and ordering, and then doing all the paperwork and bookkeeping at night."

"Sounds vaguely familiar," Roger said.

"I see why you wanted to get here early—this place must be popular," Alex said, gesturing toward the window. The parking lot was filling up quickly, and a small crowd was forming in the entryway as would-be diners waited their turn to pay.

"That's true," I said, "But in spite of the steady stream of customers, Megan has a lot of trouble making ends meet. A lack of customers isn't the problem."

"Sounds like us," Alex said. "We've got all the work we can do, but no cash."

"It's the same for a lot of contractors," I said. "This little restaurant, despite being in a small strip mall and not really convenient to anything, is packed every day. It's got great food at a fair price, but until recently,

Megan hasn't taken any money home. She's been in a slow downward spiral."

"So what you're trying to tell me is that there's nothing we can do about our situation?" Roger asked. "That it's hopeless?"

"Exactly the opposite! There is definitely something you can do," I said. "Megan is starting to turn things around, but I wanted you to know where she was just a short time ago. Her cash flow was so tight, she had to place food orders daily because her vendors put her on COD. She was taking each day's receipts to pay for the next day's food deliveries. And sadly, she was living off of the leftovers. Like that three-bean salad no one wanted that was left on the bar for three days. But she believes in what she's doing and, like you, she thought that just working harder would eventually pay off."

"I feel like I've been living off of that three-bean salad too," Roger admitted.

Labor

A SERVER CAME BY THE table to get our drink orders. Then we got up to get our food and walked to the salad bar first, avoiding the three-bean salad. Back at our table, we saw more and more people showing up, many of them wearing the same blue uniforms. I pointed out that these were workers from the plant down the street. It was a popular spot for them; they came here early to have a quick lunch before heading back to punch the clock. I explained that the next wave of customers we'd see would be mostly people dressed in casual business attire who worked at the business park a mile down the road. Later a third wave would come in, a mix of small groups of professionals and people eating alone.

"You must spend way too much time here," Alex said.

"Probably," I admitted. "But think about those guys in the blue uniforms. They come in first because they have to eat quickly, and if they can't, they don't come back. If their plant doesn't pay them on time, they won't show up to their jobs. It's the same for Megan's workers; they need to be paid on time, or she can't run her restaurant. Megan has no choice but to prioritize their paychecks to keep the doors open."

"That's just like RGC," Roger declared. "We have construction workers on payroll and we have to pay them weekly or they will disappear on us. Without them, we can't do the job. The proverbial machine comes to a grinding halt. It doesn't matter how much work we have, the equipment we have, or anything else—if they aren't there, we can't do the job."

"Exactly the point," I said.

"We subcontract most of our labor except for a few minor things, though," Alex said. "We don't actually have many laborers on payroll."

"That's common for a general contractor," I said. "In construction of any type, the lines between payroll employees and independent contractors are often blurred. The IRS has their rules, but what actually happens in construction is another story."

"Yeah, about that," Roger said. "There are definitely some blurry lines at RGC."

"We can talk about that later," I said, "but no matter what you call them, you have guys on the job who actually do the work. You may pay them differently—maybe some are on payroll and some are independent contractors who get paid weekly. Others who send you a bill may give you a bit more time to pay, but either way, the result is the same: You have a limited window of time in which to pay them, or you can't finish the job."

Suppliers

"NOW CONSIDER THE SECOND WAVE of people from the big office complex nearby," I said. "They are the core group and make up a significant portion of Megan's lunch crowd. They may not punch a clock, and their schedules may be a little more flexible, but if they aren't able to get in and out of here in a timely fashion, they won't return either."

"Sounds familiar," Alex said.

I stopped to take a bite of Megan's delicious chopped salad before continuing.

"They're kind of like Megan's food suppliers and vendors," I said. "Without them, Megan has no food to put on the buffet and nothing to sell. In your world, these are your materials suppliers and vendors."

"Yeah, we need the materials deliveries to be timely and have had some jobs delayed because they wouldn't deliver without pay," Alex said. "Whether it's concrete, pipe, fixtures, or whatever, we have terms with most of the vendors, but post-COVID and supply chain issues, we found out the hard way that we have to treat them right too."

"That was an extremely expensive lesson," Roger added.

"Those suppliers might be a bit more patient and give you slightly more time to pay, but they need to get paid too," I said. "You can't get a job done without them either."

"We usually had most of our subs pay for materials," Alex said, "but we did start paying for them too. Originally, we wanted to pick up the margin on the materials, but things changed after COVID. We got burned when the supply chain dried up and we couldn't get certain things to finish our jobs."

"We had costs skyrocket on several line items and got some late-completion penalties because we couldn't get what we needed," Roger said.

"Took some big hits there, too, so we want to start controlling some of the critical things that could derail us."

"Many contractors learned some valuable lessons from COVID and supply chain issues and changed their pricing structures as a result," I remarked. "Disruptions like COVID and the Great Recession of 2008 can teach us many cash flow lessons. Your immediate problem is figuring out how to handle cash flow differently on your jobs. For the purposes of this discussion, remember that these materials suppliers, regardless of who is buying from them, are a key component of getting the job done. They may have different cash payment terms, but just like this second wave of office workers, if they don't come back, the doors won't stay open."

"I follow you. So you picked this restaurant to tell us about waves of cash flow?" Alex asked.

"There are more lessons here than that," I said, "but let's continue."

Overhead

"Now think about that third wave," I said. "They may not be banging down the doors or on such a tight schedule, but Megan needs all the cash flow she can get and doesn't want to lose them either. She needs them to keep the doors open. They might be a bit more patient, but at the end of the day, Megan relies on them in order to afford the rent and utilities and pay for the equipment she financed to open the restaurant. Without a place to sell the food, the equipment to prepare it, and the electricity and water to cook it, she can't make a living."

"Yeah, rent, truck payments, internet, software, all this stuff I have to cover," Roger said. "Those bills just don't stop."

"Exactly," I said. "In the construction world, think of this as your overhead. Some of these bills may be less urgent to pay in terms of getting the job done, but you do have to pay them, or the gears in the RGC machine come to a halt as well. Roger, I know you can't keep the doors open without covering them. This bucket includes all the other stuff it takes to have a construction company and support your people so they can get your jobs done."

"Is this that 10% overhead factor that we are supposed to add to our jobs?" Alex chimed in. "Roger, I don't know what that number is supposed to be, but I don't think it's high enough."

"I can add up these expenses, but I still don't know how to tell my contractors what to put in their bids," Roger stated coldly. "How could I possibly know? My profit and loss statement gives me one figure, but that never seems to be enough."

"Most contractors don't know what that overhead factor truly is and are working with the wrong numbers," I explained. "Even fewer construction companies solve for that factor in terms of cash flow and continually bid with the wrong markup. Even if they bid with the right numbers to show profit on their financial statements. It's a huge game changer for contractors when they learn to bid for cash flow-based profit instead."

"I can't tell you how many times I have tried to get overhead figured out," Roger said. "I have had several meetings with our current CPA, Pam, and some so-called 'experts,' and still don't understand it. Let's talk about how I can fix that."

"You need to learn a couple more concepts first in order to get there, Roger. But don't worry, overhead isn't as hard when you think of it in terms of cash flow."

"OK, what's next?" Alex asked eagerly.

The Rotating Cash Cycle

WHEN MEGAN GETS HER FOOD delivered, she has to put it on the buffet almost immediately. It was going out as fast as it came in, and she didn't have any extra for herself or to use later in the week. Getting and paying for her supplies was a constant cash flow battle.

"This is the same battle that construction contractors fight with cash flow," I said. "Imagine a bucket with a big hole in the bottom. No matter how much water you pour in, it keeps gushing out just as fast."

"That's us," Alex said. "It is such a depressing cycle. Pam and I joke about it all the time. It's no joke, I know, but a crisis that repeats week after week. When we do get a big check, we think things will get better. Before we know it, we're back in the same boat, begging for cash wherever we can get it."

"It's like this buffet," I continued. "If all the food that comes in is put out on the bar one minute and then goes out just as fast, the cycle is never-ending. It's the same with cash flow when we have one bank account. A lot of money comes in, but a lot must go right back out. We become so reactive with our money that it becomes a revolving door. If there's anything left over besides that three-bean salad, it's a matter of chance. Not too long ago, when Megan had a little extra cash left over to take home, she ended up having to loan it back to the company."

"I know how that works all too well," Roger said.

I mentioned how the author of *Profit First*, Mike Michalowicz, uses the analogy of carving the turkey on Thanksgiving.

"We don't just pull that turkey out of the oven," I said, "put it on a big silver platter, and let everyone hack at it like Norman Bates from the movie *Psycho*. We have to carve it up and put it on different plates.

This is an imperative first step when I work with contractors and one of the core principles of construction cash flow management. I refer to it simply as 'The Accumulate Principle.'"

"Accumulate?" Alex asked.

"The idea is that you can't take all the cash as it comes in and put it in the same place it goes out from," I said. "Otherwise, it will disappear just as fast as it came in. In construction, you can have a lot of money come in at one time and feel like you're on top of the world. The next day a lot of that money goes out the door and you feel like the world is coming to an end."

"That's so true!" Alex asked. "It is feast or famine. So how do we fix that?"

"Just like the turkey, we need to carve up our cash and put it into different buckets for different purposes. We must accumulate cash in one place, but never spend it from the same place it came in. Otherwise, it disappears, and we don't know what happened."

Roger nodded. "Makes sense," Alex said.

"For many years, I told contractors to build a robust accounting system that can tell them in near real-time how they are progressing on their jobs with the goal of knowing as soon as possible if things are going off-track." I said. "As a CPA, that is ingrained in me from years of training. Quite frankly, while it is great advice for overall management of a construction business, it does not address the cash flow challenges you're facing. Generally accepted accounting principles provide a way of standardizing how to look at your finances, and consistent job costing should allow you to see where you are on your job before things go wrong and do something about it."

"Yeah, about that. We've been trying to get there too." Alex grimaced. "But we never seem to be able to pull it together. We changed software and, according to the salesman, everything should magically be fixed. Now we've been putting money into software for almost two years and feel like we are no further along."

"That's quite common," I told him. "But even with great books, cash flow is often still a problem. For many years, I told contractors *not* to run their businesses by what is in their bank account. Big money in and you tend to make spending decisions based on that big bank balance. Then it's big money out and you're caught with your pants down, without money for taxes or to cover that unexpected bill."

"Ain't that the truth?" Roger muttered.

"My epiphany came when I realized one day that no matter how great their systems are, most contractors are still going to struggle with cash flow because they manage by their bank balance regardless of what their books tell them. It is naturally ingrained in all of us to act this way. The key is that we have to change the behavior—or change the game to fit that behavior."

"OK, but how?" Roger asked, pushing away his empty salad bowl.

"Several years ago," I said, "someone came up with a game to teach these concepts that I affectionately call 'The M&M's game.' I adapted it to construction contractors and have taught it to a few hundred contractors over the years. People who have never run a business might find it simplistic and silly, but the business owners in the room always get it.

"In the game, the M&M's on your plate represent the money that you run your business with. As people play the game, they begin to understand how cash comes in and then goes right back out. They realize that we are all naturally affected by our bank balance, and when we have one account it's easy to feel like there is money to spare. When we have a lot, we feel secure. When cash is tight, we get into a reactive mode that sometimes forces us into bad decisions. Sometimes I see contractors resort to borrowing from sources they can't afford just to keep the doors open. Again, the hope is that it will all pay off one day."

"I can relate," Roger sighed.

Allocating Money

By now we were more than ready for the main course. A server had brought us big plates for the hot bar, but I left mine on the table and went back to the salad bar for one of the smaller plates. We all got our food and returned to the table.

"Why did you get a smaller plate? It's all you can eat, right?" Alex asked, smiling. "Do you feel that sorry for Megan?"

"No, I want you to understand another core principle of controlling your cash flow," I said. "In the United States, there has been a rise in obesity rates over the last few decades. There also are psychological studies that prove that when we use smaller plates, we tend to eat less and feel just as full."

"I recently lost a lot of weight," I went on, "partly by using the small plates technique. Just like carving up the turkey before we eat it, we need to split our money onto multiple plates, a separate one for each particular purpose. It's amazing to see the effect this has on your mindset."

"I have heard that," Alex said.

"So, in other words, you need to move that money into separate bank accounts, one for each purpose."

"My grandmother used envelopes for her money like that," Roger said.

"And that is where the second principle of Profit First comes in," I said. "This one I simply call 'The Allocation Principle.' After we accumulate our money in one place, we need to move the proper portions into their proper places. This simple act instantly tells us what we have to spend for what purpose and prevents uninformed spending, like Dan buying a pickup truck without knowing if the company can afford it."

I continued, "In the first round of the M&M's game I was telling you about, you have all your M&M's on one plate. In the second round, you allocate your M&M's to different plates for different purposes. What the players notice is that they spend their M&M's differently, and end up with two very different outcomes, depending on whether they use multiple plates or not. When we don't truly know how much we have to spend, pretty much all of us make choices based on our ingrained habits. Have you ever heard of Parkinson's Law?" I asked.

"No, what's that?" Alex asked.

"Most people know Parkinson's Law," I said, "whether you recognize the name or not. Essentially, it states that work expands to fill the time available for its completion. If you have two months to complete a project, it will take you two months to get it done. If you have two weeks for that same project, well, you'll be amazed by what you can get done in two weeks. Just like wrapping up a construction project. I know you both know how that works."

Alex nodded in agreement. "It's amazing what can happen when we have a deadline."

"Profit First related this principle to money," I said, "correctly explaining that it applies to any resource. When we have a lot of time, money or anything else, we tend to be freer with its use; when we have a little, we are frugal with it and watch it more closely. As a result, we make more thoughtful and informed decisions."

"I get that about time, but how do we apply this to our situation?" Roger asked.

"I related these concepts to Megan," I said, "because I wanted to help her to get out of the cycle she was in. She needed to set aside a certain amount of food in her storeroom and walk-in, so she didn't have to buy the same things again later in the week. She was frustrated because she was working day and night and not even getting a good meal out of it, but she deserved a good meal at the very least—and indeed, much more for taking the risk to be in business. I told her to make herself a plate before putting any food out on the buffet, and to start putting money aside for herself."

"I understand where she's coming from," Roger said.

"I know you can relate," I said, "and I can too. This is a concept that I personally struggled with for many years in my own business. Everyone else came first, and my paychecks were very sporadic. Accounting firms have serious seasonality problems, and it was only after understanding Profit First principles and implementing the system myself that I truly came to understand why it works so well. We can't keep playing the same game and expect to win."

I looked at Alex. "Does this all make sense?

Alex unloaded for a minute. "Yeah! I'm tired of borrowing from the next job to pay for the last one. Half the time, I'm covering the cost of other people's mistakes with my mobilization money. I'm tired of making excuses to the subcontractors and suppliers when it isn't even my company, or when my jobs have to cover for someone else's mistakes."

He paused for a moment to look at Roger, probably worrying that he had said too much.

"Continue," Roger said. "I probably need to hear it."

"Not only that," Alex continued, "I mentioned that really expensive accounting software that we've been stuck with for two years and don't know how to use. Pam tries very hard, but I don't trust the job cost information she gives me, and I don't understand how the overhead figure we use could possibly be correct."

"Alex, if you remember," Roger said, "I asked you when you came from the other company what they used for an overhead factor. It was close to our rate, so we kept using the same figure we've always used to bid the jobs since my father taught me bidding. I have no idea if it's enough. All I know is that nothing is getting better; it only seems to be getting worse. Carving up our revenue and putting it into separate buckets sounds wonderful, especially if you think that would give us some insight on cash flow and how we are spending money."

"Absolutely," I told him.

Just then, Megan stopped by the table to say hello. I introduced Roger and Alex. Alex complimented her on the food, which I knew was the biggest reward for her. Megan was proud of the food she cooked, loved her restaurant, and was gifted at making sure she knew what her customers wanted so they kept coming back.

After she left, Alex commented that she seemed very nice but looked incredibly tired.

"She's the first one here in the morning and the last one to leave. She deals with all the customers, handles all the ordering, and makes sure the quality of the food she serves is just right. She does her best to ensure that all the bills are paid. The sad part is, she rarely takes home a paycheck. She borrowed all the money she could and used her life savings to start this place. She's the hardest-working person here, yet she's always the last to get paid.

"I suppose you can relate?" I asked Roger.

"I sure can," Roger said.

"Seems Alex shares Megan's work ethic," I said when Alex returned to the hot bar to refill his plate.

"He definitely does, but he doesn't fully understand what it's like to walk in my shoes," Roger stated.

"No doubt. But he's a good one," I said.

Roger told me a bit about the promise he had made Alex before he came over to work at RGC, a loose one implying opportunity for Alex once Roger retired.

"I don't know how I can keep this promise to Alex," Roger said. "He didn't know about Dan when he started. Everyone expects me to hand this over to Dan—he is my son, after all."

Alex returned from the bar and Roger abruptly changed gears. "My turn," he said as he got up, looking at me meaningfully as he crossed behind Alex's chair—an obvious signal to keep what he'd just said on the down-low.

Order

WHEN ROGER RETURNED, I CONTINUED. "The third principle of Profit First is order. You have to do things in a certain sequence. Even if you've accumulated money in a separate account and allocated it properly, order is critical. It's one of the key aspects of running a good construction business. That's why I told Megan to fix herself a plate at the beginning of the day. After all, she is the hardest-working employee here and deserves at least a good meal, not just the leftovers.

"People think "Profit First" sounds greedy—it's not. It's about making sure you carve out profit that you can see, in cash. If you don't, you leave profit to chance, which explains why most business owners owe money to the IRS but often don't see any of the cash they owe taxes on. You have to carve out the profit before you allocate money to anything else; otherwise, it will never be there.

"Like I said before, business owners deserve to be rewarded for risking entrepreneurship. They also deserve to take home a regular paycheck and not have to pay taxes out of their own pockets. So it's important to set up separate buckets for the owner's salary, taxes, and profit in cash. I told Megan that she needed to start taking some profit for herself. If she can't learn to pay herself a living wage, she will never survive. In the meantime, she has bought herself a job that pays less than minimum wage."

Roger and Alex's mouths were full of food, and they weren't interrupting, so I continued.

"At what most business owners bring home, who else is going to do the work if you can't?"

"You're going to use that tired old 'put your oxygen mask on first before helping others' analogy you mentioned in the office," Roger said.

Alex looked puzzled, so I explained. "Alex, the idea is that the owner needs to learn to help themselves before they can build a business that helps others. So Roger, you've obviously heard this before, did you do it?"

"Well, no, but construction is…" Roger got my point and let the sentence drop.

The conversation went silent for a moment before I let him off the hook and turned back to Alex. "A contractor needs to make sure they can take care of themselves and run a profitable business that covers their needs first, otherwise they can't ensure that their employees are taken care of and that all the bills are paid. That is a lesson every business owner needs to learn."

"It's so hard to do," Roger said.

"I know it seems that way, but honestly, once you understand the principles and have your system set up—which I will help you do—Profit First will actually make it easy.

"But back to order. In the book *Profit First*, Mike Michalowicz talks about the importance of order in the context of losing weight. If you fill up on salad first, you won't be tempted to eat all that chocolate cheesecake and ice cream with sprinkles and wreck your diet. There are just certain things you have to do in order.

"Alex, when you start constructing a new building, what do you do first?" I asked.

"What do you mean?" he said. "You know what we do."

"You work on the foundation first, right? What happens if you don't pour the foundation correctly?" I asked.

Alex outlined a few harrowing tales he had heard about this over the years, sometimes even experienced. I definitely didn't have to tell this crowd about the importance of building a solid foundation.

After letting him go on for a bit, I said, "So obviously you get that you have to build the foundation before the walls. It's the same here: You have to build a business where there is not only profit to pay Roger, but also money to pay his taxes and profit to grow the company."

"I will admit," Roger said, "that I never learned how to do that. I am not only behind on my paychecks, but my taxes too."

"I had no idea," Alex said.

"So you understand now why you have to put profit first in the equation?" I asked. "Roger not only needs money to live on, but also to compensate him for the risk of being in business. That foundation has to be there for him or any business owner to be successful, much less create something of worth to others. You and Roger need to put that in order to build this company. Which leads me to my next point—"

"Anybody for dessert first?" Alex asked.

Rhythm

AFTER ALEX CAME BACK WITH a nice assortment of desserts on his plate, I launched back in. "I know I don't need to tell either one of you, with your project management experience, that certain things have to come before others in construction."

"That's Construction 101," Roger laughed.

"Construction has a certain structure—a rhythm, if you will," I said. "That rhythm is the fourth core principle of the Profit First system. When income comes in, we split it among those various buckets we talked about, using predetermined percentages. We do that in a certain order, but without a structured rhythm, the cash flow chaos will continue.

"You may have put money in a certain bucket—a special bank account for a particular purpose—but if it comes in and goes right back out, doesn't that get the same result as Megan putting food on the buffet as soon it comes in?"

"I see your point," said Alex.

"Profit First suggests what is called 'The 10/24 Rule,'" I said.

"What does that mean?" Alex asked.

"It means that you both distribute money from that income bucket into various bank accounts *and* pay your bills on the tenth and twenty-fourth of the month," I said. "That's great in theory, but it doesn't always work in construction, and you have to adapt the rule to your situation. The point is that there are important lessons we can learn from this concept."

"Yeah, I don't see how we could do that," Roger said. "We pay our people every week, and several of our subcontractors show up weekly to pick up a check too. I don't see how this could possibly work for us."

"It definitely can, and I have contractors across the country who once said the same thing but learned how to change their cash flow game. It is true that most don't follow a strict ten-twenty-four payment schedule, though. In fact, many contractors use a weekly rhythm for most payments."

"Weekly rhythm?" Roger said. "We would need to do a daily rhythm, as you call it."

"That's an important point," I said. "Sometimes a contractor is so cash-strapped when they start that they have to allocate money daily. They are used to cutting checks whenever the cash comes in, constantly watching how much money is left in their bank account and worrying if one check is going to clear too early and bounce another check. But let me ask you a question—what happens if we do allocate money daily?"

"I don't follow," Roger said. "How does that change anything?"

"Exactly," I said. "It won't change your current situation, which is the same as Megan having to buy small amounts of food every day and cook it immediately. She can't buy in bulk to save money and constantly has to keep tabs on every penny that goes in or out. It's chaos."

"So how do we get out of doing that?" Alex asked.

"It definitely is a cycle that you have to break," I said. "Implementing the Profit First system can eventually help you break free, and many contractors have to start with a daily rhythm. The problem is, if they keep doing it the same way, they stay in a reactionary state where they are so dependent on cash that they are stuck in a continued downward spiral. I want to get you to a proactive state."

"Sounds incredible, but how?" asked Roger.

I hadn't really noticed until this moment how engrossed they both were in our conversation; Alex hadn't even touched his dessert.

Temptation

BY NOW, THE LUNCH CROWD was thinning out. "I promise we'll come back to that," I assured Roger, "but first, let me tell you about the last core principle. We all need to get back soon, and Alex, you have a mound of dessert to tackle. Which is actually the perfect example of the last core principle: temptation. Alex, have you ever known anyone to go to a buffet, any buffet—here, Las Vegas, anywhere—and not overeat?"

Alex glanced down at the pile of cheesecake, layer cake, and pie he had selected from the dessert bar and laughed. "Well, you do have a point, but I have to get my money's worth, right?"

"And have you ever known anyone to go on a cruise, with all-you-can-eat food available twenty-four hours a day the entire time they are on the boat, and not gain weight on the trip?" I asked.

"True," Alex said, smiling through a bite of chocolate cheesecake.

"Let's think about the temptation of a buffet like this or a food package on a cruise," I said. "It's all you can eat, and the temptation is overwhelming. Did you know that a study found that on average, a person gains a pound a day on a cruise? If you have chocolate chip cookies in the house, they will get eaten, right?"

"Yep," Alex said as Roger nodded in agreement.

"Think about it in terms of handling money," I said. "Do you save from your paycheck?"

"I'd like to," Alex said, "but it's been tough lately with missing some checks, and my son had to get braces. Oh, and my wife's car broke down."

"It's hard to save, isn't it?" I asked. "Do you have a mortgage on your house?"

"Yes," Alex replied.

"Does the mortgage company escrow your taxes from every check?" I asked.

"Yes, the vultures!" Alex said.

"Why do they do that? Why do they add it to your monthly payment?" I asked.

"I guess I see where you are going with this," Alex said. "I have to pay that $6,000 a year at some point, otherwise I lose my house."

"And you aren't saving now?" I asked.

"I get your point, they take the money," Alex said, "and it's there when the property taxes need to be paid. Otherwise, I would be homeless. I still can't seem to save anything."

"But wait, do you have a 401(k) at RGC?" I asked.

"Yes," Alex lit up. "Yes, I guess I am saving something."

"Exactly. Why are you able to do that?" I asked.

"They just take it out of my check. I never even think about it," Alex said. "I mean, I forgot about it when you asked me about saving money."

"Guys, you aren't alone," I said. "Most Americans have a hard time saving any money and are deep in debt. The point is, if you had gotten the money in your paycheck to save for retirement or put aside for your property tax payment, would it be there?"

"No," Alex said simply. Roger watched as if it were his own son learning a valuable lesson.

"It's about temptation, whether it's your personal finances or business finances," I said. "Temptation will always be there. We have various ways of removing temptation in the Profit First system. One way is putting money into separate bank accounts for different uses. Another is using a second bank or two that aren't as accessible. Out of sight, out of mind."

"That makes perfect sense," Alex said.

A server had come by to take our plates long ago. Now she made her third visit to the table to ask if we needed anything else, like drinks to go. It was her polite way of saying she needed to clean up for the dinner crowd and would appreciate a tip.

As we walked to our cars, Alex turned to Roger and asked, "If Wade is willing, can I have him come to our pre-con meeting for the high school job?"

"Why?" Roger gave him a puzzled look.

"If we're going to pull off this job, we need the whole crew on board. In fact, many of the subcontractors may need to hear this as much as we do. We don't need one of them failing in the middle of this job." Alex said.

"Enough said—I agree. Wade, can you come to our job kickoff meeting next week?" Roger asked.

"Sure, just let me know when," I said as I jumped into my truck.

CHAPTER 3 END NOTES
Setting Up Your Buffet

CASH COMES IN AND GOES out just as fast. Sometimes we end up paying whoever screams the loudest. Obviously, we have to pay our people first or they won't come back. Our suppliers and subcontractors may give us a little more time, but we have to pay them, or we won't be able to finish our jobs. It never stops.

If you are ever going to control your finances and have money to live on and enjoy, you first need to set aside funds for profit, owner's compensation, and taxes. Otherwise, you will continue to be a revolving "lazy Susan" of cash for everyone else. That is how **you must take action** as we end this chapter.

• • •

WE WILL GET TO SEPARATING out cash in a minute, but let's quickly review the simple core principles you just learned:

1. You need to **accumulate** money in one place but not spend it from the same place.
2. Next, you must **allocate** that money to specified accounts for particular purposes in predetermined proportions.
3. Then you must establish an **order** for your allocation of the money, putting it aside for profit, owner's compensation, and taxes before you use it for anything else; *otherwise, it won't be there when you need it.*
4. You also need to make sure that cash comes in and goes out in a **rhythm** *that you can recognize and control.*
5. You do all this while recognizing that **temptation** can wreck the best laid plans, and that you must set up your system so that the proverbial chocolate chip cookies are removed from the pantry.

• • •

Action Plan

THIS STEP IS **NOT** OPTIONAL! You will set up a minimum of six bank accounts, which may require a trip to your bank. Each account should be designated with a specific purpose; as you create them, tell the bank to label them appropriately (or, if you are able to open your accounts online, label them this way yourself). They are as follows:

1. Income
2. JobEx (short for "Job Expenses")
3. Profit
4. Owner's Comp (short for "Owner's Compensation")
5. Tax
6. OpEx (short for "Operating Expenses")

You probably already have at least one bank account you can repurpose that most everything goes into and comes out of. You might have automatic deposits coming in from credit cards, and/or direct ACH or wire deposits from customers. By the same token, you may have automatic drafts, payroll payments, and/or checks coming out of it.

You must make the choice to put **all** of your income in a separate account. **This account CANNOT SERVE BOTH PURPOSES!** You cannot pay bills from this account, only use it to gather all your income, which you will then distribute in specific amounts to the other accounts in a particular order and according to a regular rhythm. (We will dig into how to do all that in upcoming chapters, but for now, the important thing is to open the bank accounts.)

It is usually easiest and cleanest to change your current account to the Income account and then ensure that all of your deposits go into that account. After you set up the accounts, you can start the process of redirecting automatic debits and payments so that they come out of the other, corresponding accounts.

I know that opening multiple bank accounts may be a bit of a pain, but just do it.

Now. Figure 3, below, will make it easy for you.

Stop reading the book and go do it. (I'm giving you permission.)

This is that moment when you start to change your path. For all the plans you've made but didn't follow through on, go do it.

For all your dreams that have seemed out of reach, go do it.

Remember where you are right now. Now think about where you want to be.

Get up, get your keys, get in the truck, and head to the bank!

Now.

I will wait until you get back.

Figure 3: Bank Accounts Planning Form

Bank Name	Account No. (Last 4 Digits)	Account Name	Primary Purpose	Account Purpose	Allocation Percentage
Bank #1		Income	Serve	Serving tray. All income is deposited here. No expenses are paid out from this account.	%
		Profit	Reward	Funds set aside to reward the owner: take first.	%
		Owner's Comp	Reward	Funds set aside to properly compensate the owner for their role in the business.	%
		Tax	Protect	Funds set aside for taxes to be paid to the government.	%
		JobEx	Serve	Funds set aside to pay job expenses.	%
		OpEx	Serve	Funds set aside to pay operating expenses.	%

PART 2

FRAMING YOUR CORE PROFIT FIRST SYSTEM

CHAPTER 4
Mastering JobEx: Core Insights for Financial Control

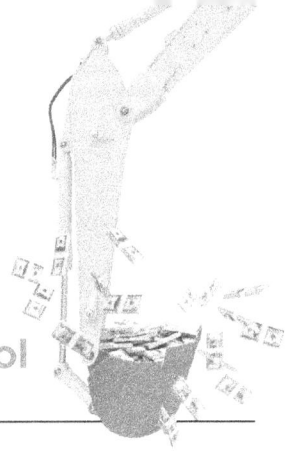

A Secret Meeting

IT WAS A COLD, RAINY Tuesday morning in January. As I walked into the local chamber of commerce building where Alex and Roger had set up our meeting, Alex met me at the door.

"Hey, come on into the conference room," Alex said. "I purposely booked this away from the office so Dan Radcliffe wouldn't find out."

As I walked in, I saw Roger and a crowd of more than twenty subcontractors who had gathered for the school job pre-planning meeting. This ground-up project was significant for RGC and many of the subcontractors, most of whom had never handled a project of this size.

RGC had set up a table of coffee and donuts, and the contractors stood around talking and enjoying those. Alex had told me that most of them knew each other and had been working with Roger's company for years.

I recognized a few of them from trade organizations and previous collaborations with Alex, like John Grant, nicknamed Elvis due to his King-like look, demeanor, and the long black sideburns he was famous for. He was a grading and underground utility contractor.

Mark Adams, who handled concrete and masonry construction, was also there. Thin, with a brown beard, he was a well-known fixture in construction circles. Both he and Elvis had been in the game for many years and experienced their share of ups and downs in the industry.

The room included subcontractors from many different trades. I was introduced to Paul Thompson, an electrical contractor whose sharp, darting eyes seemed to size up everything; clearly, he was used to troubleshooting everything on the fly. As we shook hands, I couldn't help but notice that his were rough and calloused from years of pulling wire. I learned that he had been on his own for about six years, and that Alex had been good enough to keep him supplied with work as he started his own business.

The mechanical contractor on the job, Kevin Baker, had a broad, solid build that suited his trade. His thick forearms and grease-stained knuckles suggested a man who wasn't afraid to work alongside his crew. Though I knew him by his good reputation, this was our first meeting.

Then there was Jake Morgan, a paving contractor I had met ten years earlier. He was built like a man who spent his life wrangling heavy machinery—stocky, with a perpetual sunburn on his neck and deep-set wrinkles around his eyes from years of working under the open sky.

They were all curious about my presence and why some other unfamiliar faces were there. Plus, it was highly unusual for Roger to come to these meetings anymore. This was Pam's first pre-con meeting, but most of the contractors already knew her, either from picking up checks at the office or getting her on the phone when they called, begging to be paid on time.

Alex started the meeting by thanking the group for coming, acknowledging their value as key parts of RGC's success over the years, and expressing his appreciation for each of them individually. He emphasized that this project was one of the biggest they had ever tackled and that he and Roger wanted to make it a success for everyone.

From the laughter, good-natured teasing, and inside jokes that bubbled up as Alex spoke, I could tell these people were family. The respect and trust I had for Alex seemed to be instilled in the entire crowd.

A New Approach for a Big Project

ALEX NOTED THAT THEY WERE not just renovating the school but building it from the ground up, and that this was a big chance for all of them, but also a huge challenge. Although RGC had done renovations to many similar spaces, this project required everyone's full commitment. Alex emphasized that RGC planned to run it very differently than they had in the past.

His tone then became much more serious. He said that he and Roger had talked, and Roger had his blessing to be totally transparent with them. He then shared how RGC had been the lowest bidder by 9% and explained how tight this job would be for them as a company. Then he masterfully explained how growing too fast can spell the death of a contractor because of cash flow. He mentioned how many of them had seen that firsthand in the aftermath of the 2008 Great Recession and shared some of his own previous experiences. I felt proud that he had learned from our conversations.

Alex talked about the tough years they had all faced following the COVID pandemic and supply chain issues—but he also expressed confidence that their collaboration could result in a highly profitable project that would benefit everyone if they pulled it off successfully.

He also warned of potential cash flow challenges and discussed how cash flow management was crucial for the project. He talked about how cash flow problems were common in any business, but especially in construction.

"We all know this is true," he said, "but few of us want to admit that cash flow can suck in this industry. Nobody wants to confess that things aren't going well or that they're struggling to take home a paycheck."

Kevin interrupted, asking, "Have you heard about what's going on at Precision Prime? I think they might be closing their doors. I had a job they subbed out to me and I'm afraid I won't get paid. I think the bonding company may have to finish some of their jobs."

That opened the floodgates about Precision's cash flow troubles. Once word gets out in this industry, that kind of thing is hard to hide.

"That is precisely why we need to have a conversation about this job," Alex said.

The Cash Flow Conversation Begins

THEN ALEX INTRODUCED ME. "THIS is Wade Carpenter, and he is here to talk to us about cash flow on this project."

He highlighted my years of experience working with contractors and mentioned our history working with his previous company. Then he talked about how I had been teaching him and Roger about cash flow. "I think we could all benefit from this discussion," he said.

I heard some whispering from the group and saw some worried faces. Recognizing that some of the guys were concerned about where this was heading, I started off by reassuring them that construction can be very lucrative, and that controlling their cash is the key differentiator between those who make a great living in the construction industry and those who die penniless.

I then pivoted to a discussion about Profit First and asked if anyone had read the original book or heard about it. To my surprise, three people said they had read it or listened to the audiobook. Nearly half of them had heard of the concept but didn't fully understand it.

"So how many of you have tried implementing Profit First?" I asked. Two people raised their hands and admitted that they had tried but then struggled to move forward with the system.

Careful not to divulge RGC's numbers, I then recapped some of the key points about Profit First and job expenses that Alex, Roger, Pam, and I had discussed earlier at RGC.

"We were way off from where we thought we were," Roger said.

"Yeah—with Roger's blessing, I'll admit to you all that times have been extremely tight for us. Thanks to Wade, I think we both realize now that if we don't do something drastically different to control our cash, we could end up like Precision," said Alex.

"I hate to admit it, but I've had my troubles with cash flow too," Jake said, rubbing the back of his sunburned neck. "Paving ain't cheap, and when I've got a crew waiting on a check that's weeks late, I end up floating payroll out of my own pocket."

That opened up the floodgates.

Paul shook his head, arms crossed. "It's the same in electrical. I get stuck fronting the cost of materials and by the time I get paid, the supplier's already breathing down my neck."

Kevin was next. "I've been at this a long time, and I've seen more businesses die from cash flow problems than bad work. We all know how this goes—you're running a job covering payroll and let's not forget equipment rentals, and the client hasn't paid for the last two draws."

Heads nodded around the table. No one argued. No one dismissed it.

In all the years I'd worked with contractors, I had never seen epiphanies like the ones shared among this group. I knew how hard it was for each of them to admit the struggles they faced, especially in front of this crowd they knew so well.

Once the conversation started to subside, I steered it back to the JobEx discussion that Alex, Roger, Pam, and I had started at RGC. We talked through how to get the numbers and my simplified approach for contractors with no books.

A Deep-Dive into JobEx

"THE ORIGINAL CONCEPT OF MATERIALS and subs from *Profit First* is a great way to carve out job expenses, and it's a good starting point for each of you," I said, "but the concept needs refinement for most contractors. Let's keep it as simple and well-defined as possible. The definition is simply what expenses you have—in cash, because you have a job. This needs to be clear and not subject to what accounting rules say, so let's discuss each one, starting with materials."

"Aren't materials pretty straightforward?" Kevin asked.

"They are if they are installed on or can be traced to a particular job. However, shop supplies that are kept on hand, not purchased for a specific job, should probably go in your overhead," I said.

"Easy enough," Peter agreed.

"Next—and this is connected—let's discuss the definition of sub-contractors and how it applies to your jobs," I continued. "The IRS definition of subcontractors says—"

"This fight again?" Paul asked, cutting me off. "I have this discussion with my CPA every year."

"Hang on, this isn't the same battle," I said. "I know I don't have to tell this crowd how common it is to pay people on an independent contractor basis and give them 1099 forms. The line between subcontractors and employees can be blurry. You might have subcontractors who are paid regularly and treated like employees, with bonuses at the end of the year."

"How are we supposed to compete, paying payroll taxes?" Peter asked.

"Let's forget that and the tax definition of independent contractor for now," I said. "What counts here from a cash flow standpoint is the *purpose* of your payment to someone, not the *way* you pay them. I'm not trying to be the police for the IRS. This has nothing to do with them."

"OK, help us with the definition," Alex said.

"Let's say you have a subcontractor you always pay, regardless of whether you have work for them or not," I said. "They consistently get paid for forty hours a week, job or no job. In that case, they are more like an employee. If that is the situation, I want you to treat their pay as overhead—an operating expense, not part of your job expenses."

"But my CPA says I have to put that in my job costs," Elvis protested.

"Your CPA would be right if you were doing a formal financial statement," I said. "But we are looking at your jobs from a cash flow standpoint. With that in mind, let's also take a look at people who are paid as subcontractors but don't work on jobs."

"OK," Elvis said.

"For example," I said, "maybe you paid a marketing consultant as a subcontractor, but that person has nothing to do with a particular job. In that case, you would also treat their pay as overhead."

"So how do we draw the line?" Alex asked.

"Well, let's take the flip side," I said. "If someone is on a W-2 but only works when you have jobs and you have no obligation to them when work is scarce, treat them like a subcontractor. That individual, even if technically part of your payroll, should be included in JobEx."

"So the determining factor is *why* you paid this person or company, not how?" Alex asked. "If you have the expense regardless of whether or not you have a job, it's overhead—is that right?"

"Well said, Alex," I replied.

"OK, what else?" Alex asked. "You said it wasn't just the materials and subcontractors in what you call JobEx, right?"

"Correct!" I said. "JobEx also includes other expenditures that go out in cash paid to others, and not money that you otherwise would have available to cover overhead and profit. If you wrote a check or otherwise spent money because you had a job, that is what we are after. So if that is the definition, what else would you include in this category?"

"Well, what about licenses and permits?" Alex asked. "We also have bonds on the job. Those are things we wouldn't have if we didn't have the job."

"Excellent observation," I said. "Let's take those one at a time. Licenses and permits can be a significant job expense that shouldn't be overlooked. JobEx does not include your business license or annual LLC registration because they are not for a specific job. Likewise, state or local general contractor or trade-specific licenses, though you have to have them, are not specific to particular jobs and you pay them regardless, year after year, so they are included in overhead. What would be included in JobEx are job-specific licenses and permits,"

"What about those bonds?" Alex pressed. "They were big costs for this job."

"Yes, certain bonds like those should also be part of JobEx," I said. "Costs for bid bonds or performance bonds are part of JobEx as they are job specific. The thing to look at with bonds, again, is simply whether or not you would have the expense if you didn't have the job. While you could include most things in this category in JobEx, something like a fidelity bond would have nothing to do with a job and should be considered part of your overhead and included in operating expenses instead."

"I can see this is a bit different from what I'm used to, but it seems clearer now," Paul said. "Are there any other categories?"

"There is one last category, which can also be confusing," I said. "It has to do with equipment expenditures. Generally accepted accounting principles may require allocating some depreciation to jobs, but we must pay for equipment notes whether we have work or not. Long-term lease agreements that are not job-specific should be covered by overhead. However, equipment rental specifically for a job should be included in JobEx. It can be a significant cost."

Elvis, being in the grading business with hundreds of thousands of dollars wrapped up in his equipment, had to chime in. "You mean to tell me that all of the equipment I spend money on isn't job cost?"

"It is job cost for your financial statements, yes, but we aren't talking about that," I said, "We are talking about the cash flow effect of that cost. Elvis, do you have to pay for that equipment whether you're using it on a job or not?"

"Yes, you know I do," Elvis said with a stunned look on his face.

"Then I want you to think of it as an operating expense, or overhead," I said, "OpEx is what I call it. Think of it as overhead unless you rent or buy equipment specifically for a job."

"OK, guess I'm going to have to reprogram my thinking on this," Elvis said, "but I do see your point."

"Don't worry, we will spend more time talking about equipment later," I said, "but mostly as a component of overhead, or OpEx."

I paused to look around the room. The looks on everyone's faces showed that they realized this was a different approach. I knew that for them, it must be like trying to learn a new language—when they'd never really learned the original language of job costs and overhead in the first place. A little translation was in order.

"It's OK—this is actually much easier than trying to figure out accounting rules," I said. "Just remember that we're talking about managing cash flow. We figure out whether an expense is JobEx or OpEx by asking, 'Would we be out cash if we didn't have the job?' It's that simple."

Borrowing From the Next Job

AT THIS POINT, I NOTICED that we'd been talking for almost ninety minutes without a break, so I asked if anybody needed to leave. It seemed the conversation had struck a chord with the entire group; some had jobs to attend to, but they all said those could wait and this was more important.

"Let's keep going," Alex said.

"So, I've got to say something here," Jake jumped in. "This is all well and good, but how does it help me to know what this number is, whether it's job cost, JobEx, or whatever you want to call it? I don't know what my job cost is now, and don't see what this does to change anything."

I nodded, taking in the room. Jake wasn't alone—there were more than a few skeptical faces in the crowd I needed to illustrate this concept for. "I get why you're frustrated, Jake. You're saying, 'Why does this even matter if I'm still scrambling for cash?'"

"Yeah, pretty much." Jake shrugged.

Peter Wilson, the plumbing contractor I hadn't met when I came in, was sitting in the front row. He had thinning brown hair and wore a blue company shirt that had a blue patch with his name embroidered on it.

Having met Paul Thompson on the way in, I couldn't resist. I looked at Peter and said, "Peter, don't you want to make sure that RGC doesn't rob you to pay Paul?"

"That was pretty bad," Peter said, laughing, "but yeah, I need to get paid on time. I've got to pay my guys, but materials are big too. Of course, I need to have both to get a plumbing job out the door. There usually isn't much left over."

"I get it," I said. "But do you ever borrow from the next job to pay for the last job?"

The whole room lit up with comments before Peter could respond. It was obvious from the general tone that I had struck a nerve.

"Remember when we started the meeting," I said, "we discussed the core concepts of the system, and that the first step is to accumulate income in one place—and we don't spend from that same bank account."

"We remember," Kevin said.

"So, what was the second concept?" I asked.

After a moment of silence, Alex rescued the group. "Allocate."

"Right. We have to allocate some of our income to a separate account to cover JobEx. The money you pay out in cash for expenses is really someone else's money and not yours to spend. Otherwise, you have no idea whether you have that money to spend."

"But I still have to pay my equipment notes," Elvis protested.

"Yes, but do you have that payment because of the job?" I asked.

"No, but how do I—" Elvis started to ask.

I cut him off, saying, "You cover that in your overhead, also known as operating expenses. I promise we will get to that."

Turning back to Jake, I said, "This is just the first step to you getting out of that borrow from the next job to pay for the last job cycle. This is your first step on the journey from going from a *reactive* state with your cash flow to a *proactive* state."

"You sold me!" Peter said. "So what do I need to do?"

Six Core Bank Accounts

"I WANT YOU ALL TO do two things for me after you leave today," I said. "First, you need to set up a minimum of six bank accounts. I already had RGC do this. You put specific names on these accounts. We've already talked about two of the most important ones, the Income and JobEx accounts."

Paul frowned, "Six accounts? That seems like a lot to manage, and my bank already charges me fees for the two I have."

"I hear you," I said. "It feels like extra work at first, but this isn't about making things harder. It's about clarity. Right now, all your cash is lumped together, and you're guessing what's actually available. The accounts allow for you to see exactly where your money is going."

"I get the concept," Kevin said with crossed arms, "but do we really need six? Can't we just do three to start—maybe just the Income account, JobEx, and one for other expenses?"

"Look, carving up your money into more buckets than you have now is some degree of better," I said. "But I've seen it over and over—contractors who try to shortcut the system usually end up back where they started. The whole point is to separate your cash so you don't accidentally spend what should be set aside for you to have more to take home."

Paul exhaled loudly and shook his head. "All right, what are the other accounts?"

"The other four are Profit, Owner's Compensation, Tax, and Operating Expenses, or 'OpEx' for short," I said.

"You said two things?" Kevin said.

"Right. The second thing is to calculate your JobEx as we defined it today. RGC, you have already done this exercise. How about you review it and see if you need to refine it."

"We can do that," Pam said.

"When can we get back together?" Alex asked.

///

CHAPTER 4 END NOTES
Establishing and Mastering JobEx

MANY CONTRACTORS FALL INTO THE trap of managing cash flow reactively, paying whoever screams the loudest, and are unable to follow a consistent financial strategy when it comes to cash flow. That is never going to change unless you change the game for yourself.

I'm sure there have been a few times in your life when you made an important decision—and finally acted on it—that permanently changed your trajectory. Perhaps it was the moment you summoned the courage and took the leap to go into business for yourself. Maybe it was a choice to start or end a relationship that altered your path. Do you remember a time like that?

I want this to be one of those times for you. If you are still reading but haven't done the previous exercises, it is time to get off your butt. Clear your calendar for an hour or so and go set up those bank accounts. It shouldn't take more than that, and it may be the most consequential hour you spend to change the trajectory of your business. Nothing will get better until you take action.

For the JobEx calculation, have you already done the exercise in Chapter 2? If so, you may need to refine it based on the expanded definition from this chapter. Remember, JobEx includes bonds, permits, and equipment acquired or rented specifically for the job. And regardless of whether you issue them a 1099 or W-2, if you pay people as subcontractors, their wages count as JobEx if you don't pay them when they don't work.

See Figure 4 for a worksheet to help you create your own JobEx list. Stay with me—you are making good progress now.

Figure 4: JobEx Calculation Example

	Profit & Loss	Chapter 2 Mats & Subs	JobEx Refined
Revenue	$ 1,000,000	$ 1,000,000	$ 1,000,000
Cost of goods sold:			
Salaries & wages—field personnel	25,000		
Labor—day labor	10,000		10,000
Salaries—project management	45,000		
Officers' salaries—job-related	20,000		
Materials	225,000	225,000	225,000
Subcontractors	475,000	475,000	475,000
Equipment rented for the job	25,000		25,000
Depreciation—machinery & equipment	18,000		
Equipment leases (recurring monthly)	7,500		
Bonds	4,000		4,000
Licenses & permits	1,000		1,000
Miscellaneous job costs	6,000		
Totals	$ 861,500	$ 700,000	$ 740,000
Percentage of revenue	86%	70%	74%

CHAPTER 5

Overhead Uncovered: A Cash Flow Perspective

Cold Start, Warm Reception

ALEX CALLED AND ASKED ME to meet with the group again about two weeks later. We gathered on a cold, drizzly Wednesday morning before dawn. All the same subs were there. Alex had mentioned on the phone that everyone was really excited about this discussion, so I was eager to continue the conversation with them. We were back at RGC's office, in the large conference room this time, and I wondered if Dan was going to be there.

It was early February, the slowest part of the year for many of them as well as tax preparation time. Cash flow was incredibly tight, and this weighed heavily on their minds. Working on schools is mostly seasonal; it usually happens while the kids are out of school, making July and August a crazy time for renovation work. This time, it was a ground-up build, so at least they had some work going on. Outside of those summer months, it was always a struggle for them to find the cash to fund their businesses.

When we started the meeting, I asked how the JobEx exercise had gone. As I suspected, some of the guys had an easier time with it than others. Those with formal bookkeeping systems found it more straightforward. Mark admitted that he had to go back to his check stubs, but said he'd learned a lot in the process.

Revealing the Truth About Profitability

I SHARED MY EXPERIENCE DOING the exercise on the fly at RGC with Roger, Alex, and Pam and asked them all to guess the figure we'd come up with. Many were surprised to hear that RGC wasn't making as much as they thought. Pretty much across the board, their own initial estimates were off by much more than they had expected. Though a couple of them got close, everyone had overestimated their profit, some more than others. They all agreed that it was a great learning experience and had given them a deeper appreciation for what RGC was experiencing.

"There is much to learn from this concept of seeing the world from a cash flow perspective," I said. "The beauty of the Profit First system lies in its simplicity. I want to expand on that today to include your overhead."

"If you could teach me that, it would fix several things for me," Kevin said.

As he spoke, the door to the conference room flew open and the door handle smacked loudly against the wall. It was Dan. Alex's stunned reaction showed that this was entirely unexpected. The subcontractors in the room didn't like Dan, in part because he had a history of taking advantage of them with petty back charges and fighting over change orders that he had already promised to give. Some of Alex's best subs refused to work with Dan, and it showed on their faces as he entered the room.

"Heard you guys were working on cash flow, and I figured I could help keep the ship tight on this job," Dan announced.

Defining Overhead and Its Impact

I WELCOMED HIM TO JOIN us and take a seat. "The line between job costs and overhead is often blurry, so I was trying to give these guys a definition they could follow that tracked with their cash flow. Dan, how do you calculate overhead on your jobs?"

"Dad always said to use 10% on the bids," Dan replied. "He said that's what it is and always has been in the industry. Anyway, don't mind me."

"Does anybody use a different figure?" I asked.

"I have to admit, I never really knew what overhead meant," Kevin said, "or what it's supposed to cover, much less how to measure it. All I know is, I'm in my slow season and I'm just scraping by."

"I think we are all feeling that," Mark said.

The mood was obviously low, it being the cold, dark, dead of winter. In fact, the week of this meeting had been so cold that if you went outside, your thoughts would freeze in mid-sentence. It was depressing. These guys were desperately trying to keep people employed and gear up for the big high school job. They were the squirrels who hadn't gathered enough acorns for the winter. The financial circumstances for many were so tight that they had to take out pay-by-the-week loans to cover expenses. It was obvious that these meetings had become a lifeline for them, their hope that things would get better.

"It does get better," I said, wishing they could see for themselves now what I saw in their futures. "You have been through hard winters before, but these are the building blocks to turning things around."

"As far as operating expenses, I'm not sure if I had the right number when bidding a job," Kevin said. "Job cost is one thing I thought I had a decent handle on, but overhead is something I never understood."

"What percentage did you use, and how did you come up with that number?" I asked.

"I use a 15% factor, isn't that industry standard?" Kevin asked.

"Is that industry standard?" I asked, having had this conversation many times. "Is that what the rest of you do?"

A barrage of answers came at me all at once, and I'm not sure who said what. Somebody used 10%, others said 20%, and I heard others say 7% and 18%. The highest I heard was 35%.

"OK, sounds like everyone has a different answer," I said. "How did you figure that out?"

The bombardment of answers started again. Some were based on tradition, what previous employers had used, or what they heard from peers at trade shows.

"I used exactly what my previous company did," Mark said. "I did all the bidding over there and made plenty of money. We are in the same industry, but now that I'm on my own, I never seem to cover my overhead with that factor. What am I doing wrong?"

"What you need to know is that overhead is unique to every company," I said. "What works for one might not apply to another. Different trades have different administrative costs due to their specific inputs. Even in the same trade, a large company will have a different overhead factor than a small one because they can usually spread that over more revenue. Was your previous company larger than yours is now?"

"It was," Mark replied.

"What you also need to know is that these factors change as a company grows," I said. "If you move to a higher-priced office, if you add administrative staff, it all adds up."

"I used to be embarrassed that I didn't have a fancy office," Elvis said, "but not anymore. I don't have that overhead."

Having known Elvis through his previous employer and knowing the story, I pressed him to continue. "Why don't you tell us why you feel that way, Elvis?"

He went on to explain that the company he worked for before 2008 had a lot of equipment, a nice office, and many employees. After the Great Recession hit, the company couldn't afford the overhead and went out of business. They had loans on equipment that they couldn't sell fast enough, so it continued to drain cash flow as it sat idle.

"So how do your run your business now, given what happened at that company?" I asked.

"I run my business out of my house and my truck." Elvis. said. "I realize now that I don't need a fancy office. I try to keep overhead low, but your definition of job costs from last time has me a bit confused."

"OK, forget what I told you for the moment," I said. "What is your current overhead percentage—however you define overhead—given your reduced costs?"

"I don't actually know, but it's definitely less than theirs," he said. "Given our discussion from the last meeting about equipment being overhead and not job cost from a cash flow perspective, I am now realizing why you put it that way."

Others in the room began to share details of their situations: some had offices, pickup trucks, estimators, project managers, and administrative staff.

"All of these factors are fixed costs you have to cover—so there is no standard percentage for the overhead factor; it varies based on specific company needs and operations. How do *you* calculate it?"

People around the room talked about the different methods they had used. Some had paid thousands for consultants, only to realize later that the numbers didn't make sense.

"Overhead will change over time," I said. "You could figure overhead based on last year's percentage of revenue, but new hires, software subscriptions, fuel price increases, or any additional expenses that are not in the job expenses category will affect it. As a construction company grows, overhead tends to grow at a faster rate unless you put guardrails around it to keep it from going over a cliff."

"It is impossible to control," Dan yelled, his voice cutting through the room like a firecracker. Everyone flinched, a few glancing around as if waiting to see who'd push back first. "If it changes all the time, you can't possibly come in here and tell us we can fix it. This is all a load of crap. I've seen it before and paid high-priced consultants to figure it out, but it never works."

"You absolutely *can* control and manage it," I said, "and you don't need fancy consultants to come in and tell you how to do it. We need to start looking at operating expenses from a different perspective, just as we did with job expenses. The goal is to create a simple, surrogate measure for them from a cash flow standpoint. We are not looking for a financial statement perspective that means nothing to your ability to deal with the cash. Just like the concept of 'job cost' can have different meanings depending on the users or the situation, operating expenses are subject to interpretation."

"So what are they supposed to cover?" Alex asked.

"Operating expenses cover everything money goes out the door for that is necessary to run the business but does not fall into the categories of JobEx or the other areas designed to take care of the owner, like profit, owner's compensation, and taxes. It includes things like trucks, equipment, insurance, and property taxes. Truck payments, for example, still need to be made even if they're not on the profit and loss statement."

Using a whiteboard, I broke it down. On the left side, I wrote out a typical profit and loss statement setup, listing typical job costs and sales, general, and administrative expenses sections with corresponding numbers. I then wrote down the job costs total and added the sales, general, and administrative expenses together.

Calculating Operating Expenses for Real Cash Flow Insights

"WHAT I WANT YOU TO do is add up all of the expenses on your income statement," I said.

"Then subtract the figure for JobEx that you came up with as home-work from your total expenses. Remember, job expenses are primarily materials, subcontractors, bonds, licenses, and permits, as well as equipment that you rent specifically for a job."

"What if I don't have it broken down like you do?" Kevin asked. "I have my contract labor in the bottom administrative section."

"It doesn't matter where you have it on the list—if it fits the JobEx category, subtract it from the total expenses," I said.

"I can do that," Mark said eagerly. "Then what?"

"Next, I want you to subtract depreciation and amortization from the total expenses because they aren't cash expenses," I said. "Then subtract anything you paid for yourself or on your behalf. Maybe you paid your personal taxes or your cell phone bill. Perhaps you had your wife's car on your P&L, or other expenses that are personal in nature."

"You're going to get me in trouble with the IRS," Peter joked. "My wife does my books, and she never got any training."

"I'm not here to judge your bookkeeping practices," I said, "nor do I care about what is proper for the IRS, for this purpose. What we want to do right now is recognize the cash being paid out on your behalf. One last thing: subtract the interest expense on your notes payable."

"Isn't interest expense a cash outflow?" Alex asked.

"Yes," I said, "but it's covered in the note payments we are about to get to."

"OK, so the total amount remaining divided by total revenue is the percentage we need to use to calculate our operating expenses?" Alex asked. "Isn't that what we've been doing, but perhaps with different figures?"

"That's a good observation, but OpEx isn't quite complete yet, is it?" I asked. "You are correct in that this is more the traditional, financial statement approach. So why is that a problem?"

"Um, I don't know how to answer that," Alex said.

"What is this exercise all about?" I asked.

"Cash flow?" Alex replied, sounding unsure of himself.

"Exactly!" I replied. "And—as you just pointed out—by going with the numbers on our profit and loss alone, we're using the same inputs that everyone else does. Now what we look for is what happens to cash that goes out the door. Remember I told you to exclude depreciation and amortization expenses because those don't go out in cash?"

"What else do we take out?" Mark asked.

"It is more of a question of what's missing from the definition of OpEx now, Mark," I said. "We need to go to our balance sheet now because we have cash going out there that we aren't deducting."

"I don't know how to read a balance sheet," Kevin said.

"Not a problem," I said. "If you have a balance sheet, these items should be on it, but if not, I can help you find them. First, the biggest expenditure of cash for a contractor that doesn't directly show up on your profit and loss statement is usually the amount you pay on your notes payable. Those monthly or sometimes weekly payments on your truck notes or equipment come out in cash but aren't reflected on the P&L."

"I see where you're going with this now," Alex said. "The interest is included in that note payment, right?"

"Exactly. Remember, we are looking at what happened to your cash," I said. "What I want you to do is list the monthly or weekly payments you have coming up and multiply them by twelve for monthly payments or fifty-two for weekly payments, assuming you have that many payments left in the coming year. That number includes the interest I had you take out in the previous step."

"I see why you said my equipment payments go in there now," Elvis said. "I get why you said that I have those payments whether I have a job or not."

"While we are here," I said, "just a few more tweaks to this. You may also want to look at your balance sheet for amounts paid to the owner, like distributions to pay personal taxes or draws you took to pay yourself. If that's the case, add those up and then subtract that number from your operating expense total."

"Then how do we use those figures? What can we do with this information? I still don't understand what overhead percentage to add to my jobs when I'm bidding," Alex said.

"Getting back to what you said before about coming up with a percentage, you divide the totals of each column by the revenue for the twelve-month period you are using. The numbers you end up with will be your starting allocation percentages to your different bank accounts."

"So I can use these percentages to help me bid jobs?" Alex asked excitedly as a half-question, half-revelation.

"Great insight, Alex," I said. "If you know what figure to use for JobEx, which represents the cost of the job in terms of cash flow, what happens if you bid lower than that number?"

"I'll have a cash shortfall," Alex said. "By the same token, I now know what percentage to add for overhead to estimate jobs and actually cover cash flow. So can we just use the same reasoning for our profit percentage on the job with the owner's compensation percentage when we bid?"

"You can, and that would be the minimum," I said, "but what you need to remember now is that if you bid at lower percentages than any of these figures, you will come up short on both your profitability and your cash flow. If you want more profit and to take home more money, you may need to increase that bid."

"What if I can't get those prices from my customers?" Elvis asked. "I won't get the jobs."

"Then at least you know what the jobs cost you in cash," I said.

"True," Alex said. "But what if I want to do better than those percentages? Can I use them to set targets and improve?"

"You're on fire, Alex!" I said. "Yes, that is one place we are going with this. But we need to understand where we are first, then set up and implement the system, and then we can improve. Does that sound like a plan?" I asked.

"Deal! I'm actually looking forward to this homework." Alex said as we wrapped up the meeting.

"Back to the discussion about setting up all of those bank accounts," I said. "There are more accounts to discuss in detail, but does needing all of those accounts make more sense to you now?"

"It does," Paul said.

"So are you going to set them up?" I asked.

"I'm in. I'm going to trust the process and get them set up," Jake said.

"Great! Let me know when you want to get back together and I'll see you next time," I said to close the meeting.

//

CHAPTER 5 END NOTES
Overhead from a Cash Perspective

AS WITH JOB EXPENSES, MANY contractors struggle with how to figure operating expenses and fall into the trap of thinking that overhead is a standard percentage. We will discuss target percentages in the next chapter, but remember, overhead is unique to each business. In the Profit First system, we are also defining our overhead in terms of cash flow, not just using financial statement inputs that don't reflect the cash going out the door.

Determine Your Operating Expenses (OpEx) Factor

REFER TO FIGURE 5 AS you calculate your OpEx allocation percentage. Figure 5.1 contains a filled-in example based on the sample data in Figures 5.2 and 5.3.

Here are the steps to follow:

1. Get the total expenses paid for the year:
    a. If you have a profit and loss statement, start by adding up the total annual expenses (or add the total of the cost of goods,

selling, and general and administrative expenses) and drop the number into the figure below.

   b. If you don't have any books, add up all of the bank disbursements from your bank statements for the last year. Subtract any transfers out and payments on loans to others.

2. Subtract any cash expenses that are directly tied to your jobs (your JobEx expenses, including materials, subcontractors, bonds, permits, and job-specific equipment rentals).

3. Subtract any interest expense on notes payable. (Interest will be included in your total notes payable payments in Step 6.)

   a. If you have no books, skip this step as you have already done this.

4. Subtract any depreciation or amortization expense (non-cash payments).

   a. If you have no books, ignore this step.

5. Subtract any compensation for or payments to the owner, such as salary, as well as personal payments like cell phone bills, fringe benefits, or personal auto rentals. Also subtract any payments for income taxes paid on behalf of the owner, if included on the statement.

6. Add all monthly loan payments and multiply that number by twelve months. Also add any down payments on new equipment purchased during the year.

Figure 5: Calculation of OpEx Percentage

Total Revenue

Total cost of goods sold	$
Total selling, general, & administrative expenses	
Total Expenses	

Less: JobEx expenses calculated in Chapter 4
Less: Interest expense on recurring notes payable
Less: Depreciation or amortization expense
Less: Payments made to or on behalf of the owner
Add: Annualized notes payable payments required

Total Operating Expenses $

OpEx Percentage of Revenue   %

Figure 5.1: Example Calculation of OpEx Percentage

Total Revenue $ 1,000,000

Total cost of goods sold	$	861,500
Total selling, general, & administrative expenses		128,500
Total Expenses		990,000

Less: JobEx expenses calculated in Chapter 4	(760,000)
Less: Interest expense on recurring notes payable	(3,000)
Less: Depreciation or amortization expense	(1,500)
Less: Payments made to or on behalf of the owner	(46,000)
Add: Annualized notes payable payments required	(36,000)

Total Operating Expenses $ 143,500

OpEx Percentage of Revenue   14%

Figure 5.2: Example Profit & Loss Statement

Revenue	$	1,000,000
Cost of goods sold:		
Salaries & wages—field personnel		25,000
Labor—day labor		10,000
Salaries—project management		45,000
Officer's salaries—job-related		20,000
Materials		225,000
Subcontractors		475,000
Equipment rentals		25,000
Depreciation—machinery & equipment		18,000
Equipment leases		7,500
Bonds		4,000
Licenses & permits		1,000
Miscellaneous job costs		6,000
Total cost of goods sold		861,500
Gross profit		138,500
Gross profit %		86.15%
Selling, general, & administrative expenses		
Advertising		500
Automobile lease—owner		5,500
Depreciation—office equipment		500
Dues & subscriptions		1,000
Interest expense		3,000
Office supplies		2,000
Payroll tax expense—administrative		9,000
Rent—building		24,000
Salaries & wages—administrative		56,500
Salaries & wages—officers		20,000
Taxes & licenses		1,500
Utilities		4,000
Uniforms		1,000
Total Selling, general & administrative expenses		128,500
S, G, & A expenses %		12.85%
Net income (loss)	$	10,000

Figure 5.3: Example Notes Payable Schedule

	Monthly Payment		Annualized Payment	
Line of credit	$	300	$	3,600
Note payable—truck		700		8,400
Note payable—excavator		1,400		16,800
Note payable—SBA loan		600		7,200
Total	$	3,000	$	36,000

CHAPTER 6

Setting Targets: Knowing What to Shoot For

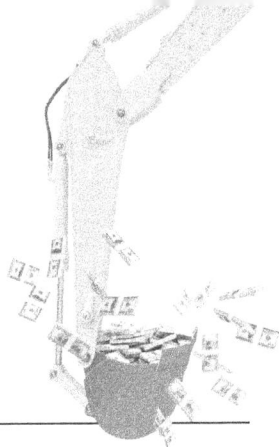

Finding Residual Revenue

"ALEX ON LINE ONE," CAME the call from Lisa, my office manager, the following Monday at about 10:30 a.m.

"Hey, Alex, how was the weekend?" I asked.

"Great!" came his reply. "Got my homework done."

"OK," I said.

"So has everyone else," Alex said. "In fact, most of us got it done by Friday, but the rest of them completed it over the weekend. That's why I'm calling."

"I'm guessing you want to set up another meeting," I said.

"Can you do it this Thursday?" Alex asked. "We're all eager to know what comes next."

"Residual Revenue," I said.

"You mean Real Revenue, like in the original *Profit First*?" Alex asked.

"Nope. Residual Revenue," I said.

"What's that? What's the difference?" Alex asked.

"You'll see," I said. "Just make sure everyone brings their numbers to the meeting. Can we do 7:00 a.m. again?"

"See you then," Alex said.

The Challenge of Overhead

WHEN I ARRIVED AT RGC's office that Thursday, it was still dark and the dimly lit parking lot was already full. Before I could get my keys out of the ignition, there was a tap on the window that would have scared me right out of my seat if I hadn't still been wearing my seatbelt.

"Sorry," Kevin said, laughing at my obvious fright.

"No problem," I replied, shaking off the heart-stopping surge of adrenaline as I got out of the truck. "Any problem with the homework? Did you learn anything?"

"It was good. Very eye-opening," Kevin replied.

"How so?" I asked as we walked toward the conference room.

"My numbers were way off from what I thought I was making," Kevin said. "In fact, I think everyone will tell you the same thing."

When we reached the door, Paul and Mark were standing there. "I need to talk to you. I have to fix this," Paul said urgently.

Before I could speak, Alex rescued me and said, "Let's take this in the meeting. Grab your coffee and let's get going."

As we got settled, Alex began. "Wade, we've been talking, and we all seem to have experienced the same thing. Some people got close with their JobEx, as you call it, but the overhead was another thing—it seems everyone was way off on that."

Before I could speak, Peter, Mark, and Kevin all tried to talk at the same time.

Alex put up a hand to stop them. "It was a wake-up call to all of us," he said.

"Like the wake-up I gave you in the truck just now?" Kevin laughed. "Payback."

"Yeah, thanks for that," I said, laughing. "What you all experienced is not surprising. As Alex said, most people have a fair idea of their job costs. However, they often don't end up making the profit they expected in their bids. Sometimes this shortfall is due to miscalculating markup. From a cash flow perspective, the real shock for many contractors is the impact of overhead costs, which are often higher than anticipated."

"Uh-huh," Elvis said, his voice dripping with that unmistakable Presley charm.

"So, bottom line, what do we do about it?" Alex said. "We are in the middle of this job."

"Exactly," I said. "You needed to know where you were starting from before you could start to fix it. Who was it who said they had read or tried Profit First before?"

"I read it," Roger replied. "Tried my version of it. I got stuck on terms like 'Real Revenue' and 'Target Allocation Percentages,' and the rest I can't really remember. I set up a couple of bank accounts."

"I listened to the audiobook in my truck," Mark said. "Never actually did anything with it. I got confused by the Instant Assessment."

A few others mentioned again that they had heard the concept but never moved forward with it or knew how.

"That is also common," I said. "There are a lot of moving parts, but the main system is straightforward once you start. Construction complicates it, and the original book does have a lot of merit for contractors, but the Instant Assessment in the book is a seventeen-step process that can be overwhelming when you add the construction job expenses. In that same assessment, you attempt to set targets. Then you go set up some bank accounts."

"My head is spinning already," Paul said.

"That's why we aren't approaching it in the same way," I said. "Believe it or not, if you have done your JobEx and OpEx homework, you have already made two major steps toward getting going. If you have set up your bank accounts like we discussed, that's three. Who has actually set up their bank accounts?"

The Missing Piece

OVER HALF OF THE ROOM had, which was much better than I had expected. Not wanting to single anybody out, I continued, "That's OK, but I hope you all are ready to do it after today's meeting. There is one major concept I want to get you to understand this morning, and that is 'Residual Revenue.'"

"You mentioned that on the phone," Alex said. "What exactly does that mean?"

"OK, so let me start by saying what the original 'Real Revenue' means," I said. "It is simply your revenue minus your materials and subcontractors. That figure, as Mike Michalowicz points out in the original book, is all you have left over to run your business. I've adapted Profit First for construction, so for us, Real Revenue is your construction revenue minus your JobEx. Your operating expenses then come out before you get to take anything home."

"I get that," Alex said. "Makes sense, but 'Residual Revenue'?"

"That's simply your construction revenue minus your JobEx minus your OpEx. Ultimately, your Residual Revenue is all you have for you as the owner, and it is split into three bank accounts. If you make a batch of chili, for example, whatever is left in the pot after you have fed everybody else is Residual Revenue. After you have paid for your materials, paid your subcontractors, and covered your operating expenses, it is all that is left for you, the owner."

"Uh-*huh*," Elvis said, his tone shifting to realization like a lightbulb flickering to life.

"OK, Elvis," I said, "since you volunteered, what are your percentages of revenue for JobEx and OpEx?"

"Uh, I didn't mean to volunteer," he chuckled. "I don't want to admit it."

"Admit what?" I asked, suspecting that I probably knew what his answer would be.

"The Colonel said my JobEx is 70% of revenue," Elvis continued, "and my OpEx figure is 32% of revenue. But that can't be right, can it?"

"The Colonel?" I asked.

"My wife. She's my bookkeeper," Elvis said.

"Well, the numbers probably are right," I said. "Anybody else get a negative number, or a smaller positive number than you thought you would?"

"I think I can speak for the group, since we've all been talking," Alex said. "Yes, that is what many of us are seeing."

"So is it any wonder you can't take home a consistent paycheck or make the profit you think you should?" I asked.

A silence came over the room as I let this sink in for a few moments.

"Remember my chili analogy?" I asked. "The Residual Revenue is what is left in the pot for you. In fact, 'POT' is my acronym for it. The *P* is Profit, the *O* stands for Owner's Compensation, and the *T* stands for Tax. Those are the three other bank accounts I asked you to set up besides Income, JobEx, and OpEx."

"How are we supposed to change this?" Mark asked.

"Yeah, we're in the middle of this job," Alex said. "We can't just make these percentages appear."

Starting Small, Scaling Smart

"You have come to a major realization in your turnaround," I said. "First, you needed to understand where you are, which you now do. Next, we'll establish some starting percentages for each of the remaining accounts: Profit, Owner's Compensation, and Tax. You may only be able to put one or two percentage points in them right now, but just remember, you can't allocate more than 100% of revenue."

"OK, so now what?" Alex asked.

"If you have your bank accounts set up properly," I continued, "all of your revenue should come into your Income account. Then you allocate money from it to the other accounts in the percentages that you just calculated. Again, the idea is that you pay operating expenses from the OpEx account and job expenses from the JobEx account and take your profit, owner's compensation, and tax amounts from the accounts set up for those."

"What if we run short?" Mark asked.

"You will run short," I said, pausing for effect. "At first, you probably will. But you will start to see what you have in each account to spend. You may naturally start to make cuts and adjustments because of that. Ideally, you won't borrow from one account to pay another. Let's be straight, it may very well happen as you get started. The goal is to not get in the habit of doing it. If you do, at least you'll be aware of it and can start taking a hard look at what you are spending money on and making some changes."

"So you are basically saying that I need to fire my administrative people and drastically cut expenses?" Mark asked.

"I'm not saying that," I said, "and I caution you against making any drastic decisions, but some of you have been operating like this for years. Some decisions have to be made over time. I want to caution you against cutting the muscle out of your company's operations. We are looking to cut the fat, but that's not just about cutting expenses. It's tough and sometimes impossible to cut your way to profitability."

"Do you mean adding more revenue to the top line?" Roger asked.

"I'm saying, add the *right* revenue to your top line: profitable revenue," I said. "That is one way. It is true that if you spread your operating expenses over a larger income base, you can cover more, but only if you don't expand your overhead expenses at the same time. That is common, but you are putting in some guardrails to help keep that from happening. Remember our conversation about needing a bigger boat? We'll discuss growth another day, but more revenue isn't the answer if you just keep doing what you've been doing."

"If nothing else, I will know what numbers to put in my bids," Alex said.

"Excellent observation, Alex," I said. "We will talk about using these numbers to find profitability. The thing you all must do now is get started with the system; otherwise, you can't begin to right the boat, no matter its size."

"I think everyone is on board with that," Alex said. "Then what? Can we set targets?"

"That will have to wait for another day," I said, "but we will get you more clarity on how you are spending and then work on the profitability. You need to manage the cash for the workload you have."

"When can we get together again?" Alex asked.

CHAPTER 6 END NOTES
Setting Targets

IT IS TIME TO ESTABLISH your Current Allocation Percentages ("CAPs," for short) and start the system. We just have a few more calculations to do. I hope you have already set up your bank accounts as I outlined in Chapter 3. In Chapter 4, we established what our job expenses (JobEx) have been as a percentage of our total revenue. In Chapter 5, we carved out the rest of the expenses that fall into the operating expenses (OpEx) category and got a percentage for that.

From here, using the same period that has been your gauge so far, we will carve out the amount left for the owner that I refer to as Residual Revenue.

At that point, we will have the initial set of numbers we need to start allocating funds and using the system.

For good measure, we will also figure out Target Allocation Percentages (or "TAPs") for profit, owner's compensation, and tax as goals to shoot for. We will calculate these with the understanding that they are not where you are right now and acknowledge that it will take time to get there. They may seem far from where you are starting out, but you can't run a marathon without getting off the couch and turning off the TV.

Please note that this is the most math you will have to do in this book. Since this step is where a lot of contractors got stuck in both the original *Profit First* and the previous derivative book on this subject, I have reengineered the process for contractors, with examples to follow, in the hopes of making it more straightforward.

My goal was to get you started on your journey, first by letting you know where you are and now by diving in with some numbers that you will improve over time.

Establishing Your Current Allocation Percentages (CAPs)

IN THE FOLLOWING TABLE, I have a calculation for you to follow along with using the numbers you generated in Chapters 4 and 5. Drop them in below where indicated:

Figure 6: Real Revenue, Residual Revenue, and Cash Commitment Base Calculation

	Your $	Your %	Example $	Example %
Revenue		100%	$ 1,000,000	100%
Less: JobEx (from Chapter 4)			740,000	74%
Equals: **Real Revenue**			260,000	26%
Less: OpEx (from Chapter 5)			143,500	14%
Equals: **Residual Revenue**			$ 116,500	12%
JobEx			740,000	74%
OpEx			143,500	14%
Total **Cash Commitment Base**			$ 883,500	88%

1. In the table above, drop your Revenue and JobEx dollar amounts from your homework in Chapter 4 onto the first two lines of the Your $ column. Put the percentage of revenue that JobEx represents in the Your % column. You can round the percentage for easier math if you like.

2. Subtract JobEx from Revenue and enter the result on the next line. This equals your **Real Revenue $.** Subtract the JobEx %

from the Revenue % to get the Real Revenue % in the Your % column.

3. Next, input your OpEx $ from your Chapter 5 homework and put the OpEx % in the column beside it.

4. Subtract the OpEx $ from Real Revenue $ to get your **Residual Revenue $**. Subtract the OpEx % from the Revenue % to get the Real Revenue % in the Your % column.

5. For good measure, drop in your JobEx and OpEx $ and % figures again on the next two lines. Add the two figures together for both the $ and % columns. This represents your **Cash Commitment Base**.

With that done, let's define these terms and how you will use them in your business.

1. **Real Revenue** represents the revenue that remains after you deduct your JobEx.
   a. This is important, because after your job expenses, this is all the money you have left to cover your overhead and then carve out some profit, pay for yourself, and funds to pay the owner's taxes.
   b. We will use this number when we calculate Target Allocation Percentages. If you want to set goals to shoot for, this is a key factor in that step.

2. **Residual Revenue** is a term that I coined to represent the amount you have left for profit, owner's pay, and taxes after you deduct both JobEx and OpEx from your Revenue.
   a. We will use this figure to establish what is left to divide between your Profit, Owner's Comp, and Tax accounts and your percentage allocation to each.

    b. You should realize that if the profit, owner's compensation, and tax amounts are not what you hoped, you will have to find additional profit by carving out percentages from the next item.

3. **Cash Commitment Base** is simply your JobEx plus OpEx.

    a. This figure, when subtracted from your revenue, equals your Residual Revenue.

    b. In the example calculation, this figure is 88% of your total revenue, leaving only 12% for Residual Revenue. Therefore, taking more money home is usually a question of raising your prices, reducing your expenses, or getting more efficient.

    c. The biggest takeaway I want you to derive from this is that working more to raise your revenue will still only net you 12% in Real Revenue *unless you work on the factors that go into it.*

Setting Your Current Allocation Percentages (CAPs)

IN THE FIGURE 6.1 EXAMPLE, you will see that we dropped 74% into JobEx % and 14% into OpEx %. This left 12%, which we allocated as follows: 1% to Profit, 10% to Owner's Comp, and 1% to Tax, equaling 100%.

Now I want you to drop in the figures that you calculated for JobEx % and OpEx %. **Please note, it is entirely possible that these two figures together could equal more than 100%.**

This happens a lot when contractors start Profit First. What I want you to realize is that you only have 100% to work with. If you are not profitable now, I strongly encourage you to allocate 1-2% of your revenue to each of your Profit, Owner's Comp, and Tax accounts anyway, with the realization that you will have to find those percentages somewhere, whether through raising revenue with more profitable work, becoming more efficient, cutting expenses, or some combination of these strategies.

Figure 6.1: Your Current Allocation Percentages (CAPs)

	Your %	Example %	Example $10K Allocation
JobEx	%	74%	$ 7,400
OpEx	%	14%	1,400
Profit	%	1%	100
Owner's Comp	%	10%	1,000
Tax	%	1%	100
Total	100%	100%	$ 10,000

Now that you have your Current Allocation Percentages (and made sure they add up to 100%), you are ready to allocate funds to the appropriate accounts. Remember, all income should be deposited in your Income account, and you must not pay any expenses out of that account.

To start, take the amount of income you have to allocate and multiply it by each percentage. Then transfer those amounts from your Income account to the appropriate accounts.

For reference, check out Figure 6.1 above, where I included an example Income account allocation of $10,000 that was allocated based on the percentages we calculated in Figure 6.

My goal is to get you to start the system, not get bogged down in the details. This part is the biggest battle for most contractors. I want to get you out of the "analysis paralysis" that often occurs when we try for immediate perfection. It is essential to actually implement the system in your business, not just think about it. Trust that you can and will improve it as you go.

So, now is the time when I need you to get off the couch and turn off the TV. If you can get this far, you will have done the hard part. *Then* you can improve upon it.

Improving your system is what the rest of this book is about.

At this point, you have a basic system to start from. The next exercise is where many people get stuck, and I don't want it to be a stumbling block. With that in mind, I give you permission to skip it if you find it too challenging. Don't make it an obstacle to getting started. If you do skip it and move on to Chapter 7, I recommend that you come back to it when you are ready because setting targets is important. Knowing where you want to go is key to making sure you get there.

Target Allocation Percentage Calculation

IF YOU ARE READY TO calculate your Target Allocation Percentages, use the calculation format shown in Figures 6.2 and 6.3, below.

Figure 6.2: Your Target Allocation Percentages Calculation

	Step 1	Step 2	Step 3	Step 4
	Actual $	Target %	Real Rev %	Allocation %
Top Line Revenue	$			
JobEx	$			%
Real Revenue	$		%	
	Profit	%	x %=	%
	Owner's Comp	%	x %=	%
	Tax	%	x %=	%
	OpEx	%	x %=	%
			Total	100%

Figure 6.3, below, is an example for you to follow as you fill out the grid in Figure 6.2. Note that each step represents a column that you will fill out in order from left to right.

Figure 6.3: Example Target Allocation Percentage Calculation

	Step 1	Step 2	Step 3	Step 4
	Actual $	Target %	Real Rev %	Allocation %
Top Line Revenue	1,000,000			
JobEx	740,000			74%
Real Revenue	260,000		26%	
	Profit	10%	26%	3%
	Owner's Comp	35%	26%	9%
	Tax	15%	26%	4%
	OpEx	40%	26%	10%
			Total	100%

1. In the second column labeled Step 1, drop in your Revenue, JobEx, and Real Revenue figures from Figure 6 (Figure 6 is reproduced below for reference).

Figure 6: Real Revenue, Residual Revenue, and Cash Commitment Base Calculation

	Your $	Your %	Example $	Example %
Revenue		100%	$ 1,000,000	100%
Less: JobEx (from Chapter 4)			740,000	74%
Equals: **Real Revenue**			260,000	26%
Less: OpEx (from Chapter 5)			143,500	14%
Equals: **Residual Revenue**			$ 116,500	12%
JobEx			740,000	74%
OpEx			143,500	14%
Total **Cash Commitment Base**			$ 883,500	88%

2. In the third column labeled Step 2, drop in the Target Allocation Percentages from Figure 6.4 below. In the Figure 6.3 example, I used the appropriate percentages from the $250K-$500K Real Revenue range. As you fill out Figure 6.2, use the appropriate percentages based on your own calculations.

Figure 6.4: Target Allocation Percentages Based on Real Revenue

Real Revenue Range ->	$0–$250K	$250K–$500K	$500K–$1M	$1M–$5M	$5M–$10M	$10M+
Profit	5%	10%	15%	10%	15%	20%
Owner's Comp	50%	35%	20%	10%	5%	0%
Tax	15%	15%	15%	15%	15%	15%
Operating Expenses	30%	40%	50%	65%	65%	65%
Total to Allocate	100%	100%	100%	100%	100%	100%

3. In the fourth column labeled Step 3, simply drop your Real Revenue percentage from Figure 6 into each one of the open spaces in that column.

4. In the fifth column labeled Step 4, do the following:

   a. Drop the Real Revenue percentage from Figure 6 into the Real Revenue row.

   b. For each of the remaining bank accounts, multiply the Target Allocation Percentage in Step 2 by the Real Revenue percentage in Step 3 and enter the resulting percentage in the column. If you wish, feel free to round to the nearest whole percent as I did in the example.

   c. The total percentages should equal 100%. If that is off from rounding, feel free to adjust an appropriate line so that the total equals 100%.

Now that you have done that, compare where you're starting from—your Current Allocation Percentages (CAPs) in Figure 6.1—to the Target Allocation Percentages (TAPs) you came up with in the Allocation % column in Figure 6.2.

Keep a few things in mind:

1. These numbers are only a guide to start from. Every business is unique.
2. In some cases, businesses have achieved better profitability than these targets, so don't treat your targets as the ceiling for your company's profitability.
3. Finally, recognize that you may currently be a long way from your target allocations. Don't let that discourage you. They may be small to begin with, but you will increase them over time as you find your own profitability.

PART 3

BUILDING YOUR FINANCIAL INFRASTRUCTURE

CHAPTER 7
Controlling Equipment Costs: Protecting Cash Flow

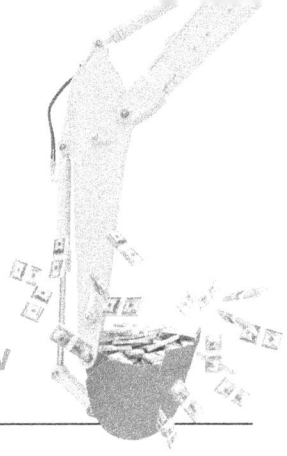

An Early Start

THE NEXT MEETING WAS IN mid-March. In the darkness of the parking lot, I stepped out of my truck and into a bone-rattlingly cold, hard wind. I was thirty minutes early, but I didn't mind coming in before the sun came up because the traffic was lighter. I found out long ago that I am wired like the contractors I work with—I'm an early riser and, like them, do my best work in the morning—so I wasn't surprised to see several pickups already there.

By now, I mostly recognized which pickups belonged to which guys. I spotted Elvis's silver truck, distinguishable by its Graceland bumper sticker and the Elvis bobblehead on the dash. He hopped out and walked toward me.

"Morning," he said. "Could I pick your brain?"

"Good morning. Sure, what's up?" I asked.

"I've been struggling with one part of the JobEx calculation," Elvis said as we walked toward the side door. "I still can't wrap my head around your approach to equipment and not counting it as a job expense, which has always been drilled into my brain. My CPA would probably disagree with you, and I don't understand why or how you could even suggest it. I buy all of my equipment unless I have some kind of emergency. You don't understand how critical it is to this industry."

"There's no doubt that grading equipment can be incredibly expensive," I said. "If we're talking about your financial statements, then I absolutely agree with your CPA, it is job cost, and the accounting rules are pretty clear on that. What we are talking about here is what happens with your cash flow."

"I still don't understand why you categorize equipment payments as overhead unless I rent specifically for a job," Elvis said. "I often rent several pieces of equipment before buying them on a long-term lease. The dealer makes it so easy to get financing, and the payments are cheaper than renting."

We entered the conference room, poured ourselves some coffee, and nodded hello to the other early birds as we continued our conversation.

The Reality of Equipment Cash Flow

"THESE LONG-TERM LEASES," I SAID, "when not tied to a specific job, are fixed costs you have to pay even if the equipment isn't being used. I know the cash outlay can be huge. If that equipment sits idle, it's costing you money, right?"

"Uh-huh," Elvis said.

"Then it is clearly an operating expense," I said. "On the other hand, equipment rented specifically for a job you can return and stop paying for, right?"

"Uh-huh," Elvis said. "So I've got to set all this money aside in OpEx for the lease payments? I've been saving to cover them, but I've also got these huge repair bills, fuel costs, insurance, and interest on the machines."

"I totally understand that for your type of construction, equipment expenses can be significant. I guess I need to explain more about my concept of JobEx, especially for contractors like you and our paving guy who have such a big investment in equipment."

"I had to make some repairs recently," Elvis said, "so I also want to talk about how expensive major repairs can get. I've been doing this long enough to know that they come out of the blue. Every time I think I have cash to take home, something breaks."

"I completely understand," I said. "That's why I often recommend setting aside some funds from OpEx in an additional bucket for what I refer to as capital expenditures, or 'CapEx.'"

"Bucket?" Elvis asked, "You mean another bank account?"

"Yep," I said. "CapEx can add up fast, especially for your type of construction. A pickup truck can now cost over a hundred thousand dollars, so it's easy for this category to drain a lot of cash."

"Yeah, I do a lot of highway work and have to maintain my equipment during the slower times of year," Jake said, walking over and taking a seat. He was the paving contractor on the job and had missed some of the meetings, but he'd gotten pulled back in after hearing the other contractors talk about the progress they were making.

"I get it," I said.

"During the busy times," Jake continued, "my crew needs that equipment in top shape. I invest hundreds of thousands of dollars in it, but if a machine is down, I can't make money."

Elvis said, "Yeah, I've been trying this Profit First method, but I immediately had to raid my OpEx because we had an unexpected repair on one of my biggest excavators."

"Jake, I was just telling Elvis that for companies with major equipment needs, I recommend carving out another bank account from OpEx to gain more clarity on how you are spending money in this category. The original *Profit First* book tells the story of Ernie, Mike Michalowicz's landscaper. Ernie bought equipment to fix Mike's chimney and gutters—justifying the purchase by saying he might use it *someday*. The point is that sometimes we justify buying more equipment because we think it will give us additional revenue options for the future. Ultimately, it can end up straining our finances."

Impulse Buying vs. Long-Term Planning

"WELL, I GET THAT. I love going to the equipment auction," Jake said.

Elvis nodded. "I love a good auction too."

"The goal of a Capital Expenses—CapEx—account," I continued, "is to address these kinds of expenses. Different types of construction have varying needs, but for many contractors, buying equipment can become almost like an addiction. While you might have lower out-of-pocket costs than you would if you were renting, once you factor in maintenance and insurance, the difference is less significant than you might think. The idea is for you to set aside funds to cover these expenses so that you don't disrupt the cash flow system you've worked hard to establish."

"But that doesn't help me when unexpected repairs wreck my cash flow," Elvis protested.

"We all know that repairs, including some major ones, will happen," I said. "Even with careful planning, these costs are a fact of life. Replacing vehicles is inevitable too. I'm guessing you both probably run the wheels off of yours."

"Got almost 80,000 miles on mine and it isn't a year old yet," Jake said.

"Sure," I said. "And also, everyone believes they need more stuff. It's common for contractors to buy another truck at the end of the year to reduce their profit so they don't have to pay as much in taxes. The goal is to have control over your spending on capital purchases and ensure that you're setting aside enough to cover these costs."

"Yeah, but the more equipment I have, the more money I make," Jake said.

"About that," I said. "Do you really make more money? It's a great tax write-off, but have you ever looked at your debt? Is it growing each year? Are you building wealth?"

"I made money last year," Jake said.

"Me too," Elvis chimed in. "At least, my CPA said I did when I did my taxes."

"So how much did you take home last year?" I asked.

"Well, not as much as I'd like," Elvis said. "In fact, the Colonel is pretty pissed at me because we're behind on our mortgage. Cash has been a little tight, especially through these winter months."

"Exactly," I said, "and we do need to talk about seasonality. But my point is that we need to plan for capital purchases and stop impulse buying. You may come across a deal on some equipment; I'm not saying you shouldn't get it. The question to ask is, should you buy something because it's a deal you can't pass up and then struggle to make payroll? Is it worth it to wreck your cash flow spending money you don't have?"

"Yeah," Elvis said. "I've been guilty of that. But all of this will pay off one day."

"Hopefully, but shouldn't one day start sooner rather than later?" I asked. "What if that day never comes?"

"Yeah, but I've been building my business over time," Elvis said. "I hope to be able to retire one day."

"How long have you been doing this?" I asked.

"Over twenty-five years now," came Elvis's reply.

"And you're still not taking home a regular paycheck?"

"Well, yeah," Elvis said, "but I should be able to sell my equipment. Plus, hopefully someone will buy the company from me."

"Remember your previous company?" I asked. "A lot of my guys, especially in the grading and heavy equipment trades, didn't survive 2008."

Elvis looked at me sheepishly and said, "Yeah, I remember."

"So what's different here?" I asked. "If you're constantly in debt, like the people who got caught with their pants down back then, what happens if you don't have work?"

"Yeah, I know that all too well," Elvis said.

"And if you aren't taking home a consistent paycheck, why would someone else want to buy your business?" I persisted.

"I guess I just need to get more projects and work harder," Elvis said.

"How do you do that?" I asked.

"I can lower my prices," he answered with a grimace.

"That's precisely the point," I said. "If your price goes below what you can really afford to do the job for, then ultimately, you're in a never-ending downward spiral.

"Back in 2008, a bunch of residential work dried up. Don't you remember what happened after that?"

"Yeah, everyone was undercutting bids," Elvis said. "All the residential graders tried to jump on commercial jobs, so more people were bidding, which drove the price down. They were just trying to keep their equipment and their people, but as a result, we started bidding lower than we could really afford. I see your point. You win."

"Nobody wins when this happens," I said. "And your comment about things paying off one day when you sell your equipment—hopefully you can sell it for more than you owe on loans for it and clear some cash. But again, what happened during the Great Recession? Everybody dumped their equipment at once so it wasn't worth a fraction of what they would normally have been able to sell it for."

"The company I worked for had to come out of pocket just to sell off the equipment," Elvis said. "They owed more than it was worth."

"Given that, do you really think you can count on it paying off for you?" I asked.

Elvis shook his head. After a moment of awkward silence, Jake asked, "Do you think we should just rent all of our equipment all the time? It's going to cost more money."

"No, that's not necessarily what I am saying," I said. "But you do also have to weigh the cost of that equipment sitting idle. If equipment is a cost of doing business, you need to plan for it. Planning for it means knowing what it costs you in cash flow and, ideally, having money set aside to cover payments, maintenance, times when it sits idle, *and* major repairs. If you don't, maybe you should hold off on that purchase."

"I see your point," Jake said.

Paul, who had walked up behind me and was listening to the conversation, jumped in. "OK, so how do I deal with slow times and getting hit with unexpected repair bills?"

"Seasonality has already come up this morning," I said. "That is a major problem in construction, and I get that we need to address it. Let's finish talking about planning for both expected and unexpected expenses with regard to our equipment, though."

"I don't have a crystal ball any more than you do," Jake said. "How can you plan for the unexpected?"

"There's obviously no foolproof way," I said. "But if we have no plan, meaning no reserves in the bank, we'll always get caught with our pants down. Jake, you mentioned that you were hit with fixing highway paving equipment. You spent a lot of money on that, right?"

"Yep, especially during the busy season," Jake said. "We need that equipment working and I can't afford to have it go down. We spend money on maintenance and repairs during our slower times because we must. Unfortunately, that's when our cash flow is the worst."

"Yeah, we try to do maintenance as well," Elvis added, "but probably not in as structured a way. We do it when we have to, but it does mean that sometimes we're out of commission."

"Obviously, things break no matter how much maintenance you do," I said. "The goal is to not completely wreck your cash flow when something like that happens. We need to put money aside for it."

"That's pretty obvious," said Jake. "But how?"

"There's no one right way," I said. "As a road and highway paving contractor, you may have that dialed in pretty well."

"We have planned expenditures every year," Jake said. "We know when it's coming, though it's always a hit to cash flow at the time we need it most."

"Yeah, I wish I had the money to take care of that in the slow season," Elvis said, "but I can't afford to when cash isn't coming in."

"We need to make sure we have the money. And guys, like I told Elvis earlier, for contractors who deal with this, I suggest adding another bank account to set aside the funds. Remember, that money needs to come out of the OpEx money we've already set aside. Let's say your OpEx is 30%. If, for example, 6% of that is spent on repairs, maintenance, and buying new equipment, you should set that money aside so it's there when you need it."

"If I don't have the cash flow right now, how in the world am I supposed to do that?" Elvis asked.

Creating a Drip Account for Stability

"You need what I refer to as a Drip account," I said. "You may have one or more Drip accounts to cover both expected and unexpected repairs or maintenance. For every dollar that comes in, just drip a certain percentage of it into the account over time. Then you don't have to borrow money and spiral deeper into debt."

"That sounds like wonderful practice," Elvis said, "but how can I get started with it if I don't have enough now?"

"Would you miss 1% or 2% off the top of every check?" I asked. "Could you set that aside? Sometimes all it takes is just a couple of percentage points, if you do it consistently. It may not be enough for the first year or two; but having even a little money set aside can help you avoid taking out one of those outrageously expensive loans. The key is to start and then stay consistent. Over time, it gets easier to build your savings and avoid tough situations. Just start by setting aside a fixed percentage of every dollar that comes in as income."

"What number do I use?" Jake asked. "I don't know what I'm shooting for."

"Start by looking at what you spent on repairs and maintenance last year," I said. "Then review the truck fleet and equipment costs that you are trying to cover. Do you have some scheduled repairs? How much will they cost? Do you have some planned expenses? Do you need to replace a truck in the coming months? Just ask yourself, 'What is the total dollar amount that I need to cover?' Then look at the total revenue you expect for the year and use that percentage."

"That sounds doable," Jake said.

"Do we only use the money for equipment expenses?" Elvis asked. "If it's built up in there and we have some other unexpected expense, can we use it for that?"

"If you constantly raid that bucket for expenditures that have nothing to do with it, you'll never learn to control that spending," I said. "It does take some discipline, but you will find that simply having it in a separate bank account helps with the temptation. It may not stop you, but if you raid the account, at least you realize that you're doing it."

"I completely understand," Jake said. "Like you said, it's probably not going to be enough the first year."

"There will always be unexpected hits in business," I said. "Quite frankly, it will never be perfect. But every year, your cash flow will become clearer and easier to manage. If you've got funds set aside for buying and replacing equipment, you at least have some kind of guideline for what you can spend and still take home what you planned to take home."

"Sounds great," Jake said.

"Another thing you might want to do," I said, "is keep a separate ledger—it can be just a simple spreadsheet—to track money dripping in and out of the account. If repairs are a big expenditure, create a separate spreadsheet of planned expenses and list how much you think they will cost. That way, you'll know what's coming as best you can."

"We have something like that on our maintenance schedule," Jake said. "I could use that."

"Right," I said. "If you see that you'll need a major repair four months down the road, at least you know that you'll have a shortfall and can plan for it. As you start to implement Profit First over the next weeks and months, you'll be able to protect your cash and have a lot more clarity on your financial status moving forward. Does that help?"

"I'm going to the bank to set up that Drip account after we leave here today," Jake said.

//

CHAPTER 7 END NOTES
Controlling Equipment Costs

THIS CHAPTER MAY OR MAY not apply to you. If you are a general contractor and don't perform a lot of work that requires equipment, CapEx and Drip accounts are entirely optional. Grading contractors with hundreds of thousands of dollars' worth of equipment should probably consider opening one or both of these accounts.

Essentially, this is a refinement of the basic system. It can help clarify your overhead even further so you know how much of your money should and is going toward equipment. It can be a good budgeting tool as well as a control on the addictive behaviors some contractors seem to have around "investing" in their companies.

I fully understand buying equipment just to ensure that you don't pay taxes. And, if you are not taking home the amount of profit you think you should, I want you to consider how much you are spending on this category.

Given the extensive calculations in Chapter 6, I will make these follow-up notes short and simple and leave you with an example "Drip" account (Figure 7, below) that you can use as a template if you do decide to carve out another bank account for this purpose.

Figure 7: Sample Equipment Drip Account

Date	Description	Deposits	Withdrawals	Balance	Notes
1/10/2025	Initial Allocation Deposit	4,965.00		4,965.00	Initial allocation
1/24/2025	Allocation	2,900.00		7,865.00	Allocation
2/10/2025	Allocation	1,520.00		9,385.00	Allocation
2/15/2025	Maintenance Expense		780.00	8,605.00	Maintenance, oil change & inspection
2/24/2025	Allocation	6,165.00		14,770.00	Allocation
3/2/2025	Vehicle Down Payment		5,000.00	9,770.00	Down Pmt: For new work truck
3/10/2025	Allocation	1,655.00		11,425.00	Allocation

CHAPTER 8

Debt Discipline: Balancing Leverage and Cash Flow

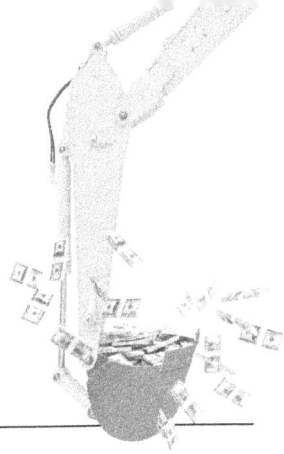

The Debt Dilemma

As our conversation about equipment wound down, I noticed that the rest of the crowd had gathered to listen. I glanced at my watch and saw that it was almost fifteen minutes after we were supposed to start the meeting.

Elvis, wanting to continue, asked, "So you mean I'm not supposed to have any debt for equipment, or anything else? There's no way I can do that!"

"I didn't say that you shouldn't have debt," I said. "Quite the opposite. When it's used properly, debt can be great leverage for taking your company to the next level. But if it's misused or you take on too much, it becomes—"

Alex, who had been listening intently, cut me off. "OK, you know what, let's take our seats. Sorry, Wade, I can't wait to hear this, but I do need to get some things out of the way." He started the meeting, which gave me a chance to refill my coffee cup and sit down.

Project Pressure and Cash Flow Priorities

First, Alex went over how the job had been going. He told us that the county was really pushing to make sure the project was finished in time for the next school year and had even reminded RGC of the late-completion penalty on the project. "We're a little behind right now, guys," he said, "and I'm going to need everyone's help to get back on track."

Precision had been doing another school renovation job for the county, but ultimately, the school board had to bring in the bonding company to finish that job because Precision couldn't. Alex said he had used Precision's situation as an example to make sure the county understood how critical cash flow would be to this project. They told Alex that they understood and would do everything they could to make sure RGC was paid in a timely fashion so they could get the school finished on time. I was proud to hear how he had explained the cash flow situation to the commissioners.

He went on to tell the group that while the job budget was tight, they all had the luxury of the job being in their backyard. As a result, they didn't have the out-of-town living and per diem expenses that Precision had been faced with. Then he mentioned his history with the architect, who was famous for questioning and cutting pay applications; he didn't want to give the guy any excuses to hold up cash flow.

"But no matter what, folks, you are each crucial to the success of this job. I want to thank you again for prioritizing it," he smiled.

From the nods, cheers, and slaps on the back the crew responded with, I could tell that the feeling was mutual. It was apparent that they truly appreciated his openness and feeling like they were all part of a team.

The group discussed project schedules and requirements, upcoming inspections, and which jobs had to be finished first. Alex passed around Gantt charts and artfully coordinated timelines for when each subcontractor should expect to be needed. He reminded everyone to get their pay applications in on time so that RGC could get theirs to the county by the twenty-fifth.

Breaking Free from Debt

As THEY WRAPPED UP THAT part of the meeting, Peter, the plumbing contractor, jumped in. "Can we get back to the debt discussion? My debt load is killing my company right now, but I need all the equipment, and I'm stuck. I've got to get a handle on it to keep things running."

"We've got all these trucks to pay for, and it feels like there's no end to it," Kevin said.

Having covered all of his major points, Alex asked me to come up and continue the conversation. The comments kept coming as I made my way toward the front of the room.

"During COVID, supplier prices skyrocketed," Paul said. "I ended up putting a lot on my line of credit, and now I just don't know how to get out from under it."

"You didn't run that debt up overnight, right?" I asked.

"No," Paul replied.

"So you're not going to get out of it overnight either," I said. "There's no magic red pill you can take to instantly change your world. You can, however, make serious progress quickly if you manage your debt properly and have a plan."

"OK, so how do we do that?" Roger asked.

"What do you do when you have credit cards or other debts?" I asked.

"I pay the minimum monthly payment," Mark said. "I know that doesn't help much, but it's all I can afford."

"Exactly. People pay the minimum and hang onto their debt for years. But remember, we're carving out a certain amount of money for operating expenses, and debt payments are an operating expense."

"When we pay off a note, like a truck loan," Mark observed, "it's like a weight has been lifted from our cash flow."

"Right, but what do we do with that freed-up cash?" I asked. "It usually gets spent on other things and just disappears. But what if we kept making those payments even after the debt was paid off and just applied them to other debts?"

"That makes sense," Mark said, "but easier said than done. I've got some high-interest credit cards to pay down too."

"Have you guys ever heard of Dave Ramsey?" I asked.

"Debt snowball!" Alex said from the back of the room.

"Exactly," I said. "Ramsey didn't invent the concept but is well known for it. It suggests paying off the smallest debt first, regardless of the interest rate. The idea is, if we keep putting the same amount toward our debt, we can start to tackle the principal more aggressively. It's also motivating and builds momentum that can be transformative. The debt snowball approach can make sense. The key is to look at your situation and decide what works best for you."

"So how do we implement that in the system we are building?" Alex asked.

"The spin with Profit First is that we take our profit at the end of each quarter and do something productive with it. If you're deep in debt, you might want to put 95% of it toward your debt. Throwing a good portion of your earnings at your debt can knock it down faster. But as the owner, you should still reward yourself with some of that profit."

"That makes a lot of sense," Mark said. "But how much debt is too much?"

"It depends on your circumstances, but banks start to get nervous if your total debt exceeds three times your equity. Working capital is crucial if you want to borrow money or are trying to make your bonding companies comfortable with your situation. Focusing on current debts before trying to borrow more can help dress up your financials."

"So how do we figure out a plan?" Alex asked.

"As you might guess, I've got some homework for you." I said. "I want you to simply create a list of all your debts—notes payable, credit cards if you're not paying them off each month, and other lines of credit. Include all of it, along with the required monthly payments for each. You may already have done this when we reviewed operating expenses. Your list will at least show you what you need to cover every month."

"That might be scary to look at," Kevin said.

"It might," I said. "Not as scary as someone jumping out at you in a dark parking lot, but I get it. I tell contractors to put that list in a spreadsheet and then set an order for paying down the debts, with the goal of freeing up operating cash."

"Again, scary, but I like it!" Kevin remarked.

"There are a few reasons to do this," I said. "Not just to free up cash. I also want you to think about building wealth. Remember, you need profit to pay off debt, so you might reconsider buying equipment just to knock down taxes. Carrying a lighter debt load also puts you in a better position to take advantage of opportunities."

"How do I make sure I don't get into this mess again after I pay off my debt?" Roger asked.

Guardrails for Financial Control

"The Profit First method and the modifications we've already made to the system will help with that," I said. "The behaviors behind the system constrain your cash flow so you naturally get to a place of knowing what you have to spend. Which makes you think twice about buying something you can't afford, especially when something like payroll is on the line."

"Like when Dan went and bought a truck just because we got a job," Alex said.

"Exactly," I said. "He didn't understand how tight cash was and didn't appreciate the situation.

"Also, you're going to hide some of your money from yourselves by putting profit and tax funds in holding accounts at a different bank to reduce temptation. When you implement these cash management controls, you start seeing a change in your behavior. I think some of you are already noticing that."

"I know we have," Alex said.

"Yeah, I've started to see a little show up in my Profit account," Paul said. "It's encouraging to watch it grow, but I've been tempted to spend it. I figured you'd fuss at me."

"It's not about right or wrong," I said, "and nobody is going to browbeat you; it's about you recognizing the behaviors and having guardrails around your spending. Even if you kick yourself later for spending, you at least recognize that it can destroy your cash flow and best-laid plans. Whether you realized it at the time or not, hesitating because you knew you didn't have the money to spend may have kept you from making a bad or impulsive decision," I explained.

"The truth is that I've never really had a cash plan," Roger said, "or known how to even begin to control it."

"As you grow, your needs and overhead will increase," I added, "but we'll keep that in check. We'll talk more about that later. For now, understand that the constraints we're putting into place will help prevent things from getting out of control again."

"Sounds like a game plan," Elvis said.

CHAPTER 8 END NOTES
How to Get Out of Debt

DEBT CAN BE A USEFUL tool to help your business grow, but it can also cause big problems if not handled carefully. Many contractors use debt to pay for equipment, trucks, or large projects. While this can help your business expand, taking on too much debt can make it hard to keep cash flowing and cover important expenses.

The key is to only take on debt with a clear plan for paying it back. If debt isn't managed well, it can eat into your profits and leave you stuck making payments for years. Think of debt as a tool to help your business, not a quick fix. Use it wisely and make sure it fits your long-term goals. With the right approach, debt can help you move forward without being a drag on your business for years to come.

The debt snowball is a simple way to get out of debt that works by focusing on small wins. First, make a list of all your debts, starting with the smallest balance and working up to the largest. Then pay the minimum amount on all your debts except the smallest one, putting as much money as you can toward paying it off. Once that first debt is gone, add the money you were paying on it to your payment on the next smallest debt. This creates a "snowball" effect as you quickly pay off more and more debt.

This method works so well because it's motivating. Paying off one debt feels like a win and gives you confidence to tackle the next one. It doesn't matter if the smallest debt has the highest interest rate; what matters is building momentum. Over time, this process helps free up cash that was tied to minimum payments, giving you more money to attack the larger debts. It's a simple plan, but one that can make a big difference in how quickly you get out of debt.

The debt snowball works even better when you combine it with Profit First. When you take your quarterly profit, you can use most of it to pay off your smallest debt while keeping a small amount as a reward for yourself. This will help you pay down debt faster while still allowing you to celebrate your progress. By focusing your profit on the debt snowball, you stay motivated and make real progress toward becoming debt-free.

One way to avoid falling back into debt is to set up controls on your spending. Profit First helps by giving you clear limits on how much you can spend. Separating your profit and tax money into accounts at another bank keeps it out of reach so you're less likely to spend it on other things. These simple steps make it easier to stick to your plan and avoid bad financial decisions.

The first step to getting out of debt is knowing exactly what you owe. I have given you a format to follow in Figure 8 below. Start by listing all your debts, including loans, credit cards, and lines of credit. Write down the total balance, the monthly payment, and the interest rate for each debt. Seeing it all in one place can feel overwhelming, but this is an important step toward helping you understand what you need to pay each month and plan to tackle it.

Once you have your list, decide which debt to pay off first. The debt snowball method works by starting with the smallest balance, but you can focus on a high-interest debt if that makes more sense for you. The goal is to free up cash as you go, making it easier to pay down the rest. Stick to your plan and you will build momentum that ultimately helps you save for the future, take advantage of opportunities as they arise, and take more profit home.

1. Fill in the Debt Type column below as follows:
   a. Enter "CC" for credit cards
   b. Enter "LOC" for lines of credit
   c. Enter "Fixed" for fixed-term loans
   d. Enter "Revolving" for other revolving credit that does not fit into the previous categories
2. Due Date refers to the day (or days) of the month the payment is due.
3. In the Payment Frequency column, enter the frequency with which your payment is due, such as:
   a. Monthly
   b. Weekly
   c. Daily
   d. Quarterly
   e. Annually

Figure 8: Debt Analysis

Bank/ Lender	Debt Type	Balance Owed	Interest Rate	Minimum Payment	Due Date	Payment Frequency

CHAPTER 9
Creating Clarity: Considering Your Banking Needs

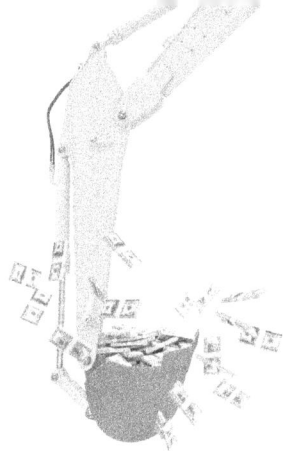

The Pushback on Bank Accounts

As I WALKED INTO THE conference room for our next meeting, I was pleased to see that Pam had joined us. As RGC's accountant and controller, she was the one dealing with all these changes and trying to keep the books straight. I said a quick hello to her before the meeting started.

"I don't have much to go over with the job," Alex said, "But I was told that there are some special questions today. Wade, we're going to get right into it if that's OK."

"Sure," I said as I made my way to the front of the room. "How are things going? Any thoughts from last time on equipment or debt? Has everyone gotten their bank accounts set up and started allocating money?"

"I don't understand why you're creating all these bank accounts," Pam said as soon as I got the words out. "You're just giving me more work."

"It shouldn't be that way if you follow the process correctly," I said, "but there are some tricks to know."

"Alex explained a lot about cash control and the new bank accounts," Pam said, "and I'm trying to keep an open mind, but the bankers wanted an explanation and I'm just thinking about reconciling all of those extra accounts."

"Yeah, I've been wondering the same thing," Paul said. "Why make things more complicated?"

"I've had people questioning me as well," Peter said. "It feels like having more accounts just means more chances to make mistakes."

"I'm worried about the additional bank fees," Mark said. "My bank charges monthly fees for each account. This is going to get expensive."

"I'm trying to grow my business," Kevin said, "but I don't need extra costs eating into my margins. How do we keep these fees under control?"

Managing Bank Fees and Banker Relationships

"WAIT, SLOW DOWN," I SAID. "Not all banks are friendly to Profit First, but some work with it very well. In one case, I talked to the banker for my client and, once they understood what they were doing and why, they looked at the whole relationship and waived most of the fees to keep the client. I'm not saying that will happen to you, but sometimes it's not a bad thing to review whether your current bank is actually taking care of you."

"Aren't we just creating more transactions?" Pam asked. "Won't the balances be smaller if we split them up?"

"True, you will keep less money in each account," I said, "but you're still maintaining the overall relationship. If you've been a good customer, you can sometimes negotiate those fees down too. Do your homework and you might find banks that charge little or nothing for extra accounts. I work with some local and internet banks that have completely free checking accounts."

"What do I do about them looking at me sideways for having so many accounts?" Peter asked. "They probably get some kind of commission or incentive for opening them, right? They should be happy to take my money."

"I once had a client bring a copy of *Profit First* to the bank with them when they started the system," I said. "They used it to justify their reasoning for adding the accounts, so if that works for you, do it. To be honest, most bankers really don't have a problem with it; it's usually more about self-consciousness on your part. Either way, it's an opportunity to build a good relationship with your bank or find one that wants that relationship."

"It wasn't a problem in my case," Pam said. "They were glad to set up the accounts and said something about it putting them over the top for the month so they would get a bonus."

"Again, it usually isn't the bankers," I said. "When they see you handling your money responsibly and understand why, it can open some doors. In one case, it led to the expansion of one of my client's lines of credit."

"But all of that reconciling," Pam said.

"Believe it or not, I have close to twenty bank accounts in my accounting firm," I said, "and each one serves a purpose."

"You're not right," Pam joked.

"That's what my wife tells me," I said. Everyone laughed. "You may not need twenty bank accounts, but multiple accounts are a great way to control your money. That's actually part of what I want to discuss today. If you have specific purposes for more accounts and they give you clarity on your spending, adding them can be useful."

"Again, I'm trying to keep an open mind," Pam said.

"The reconciliations are much easier than you would think, but can we come back to that in a bit?" I asked.

"Sure," Pam replied.

"Let's discuss other scenarios where you might want to add accounts beyond the core six. We talked about a couple last time, for equipment and debt. Can you think of any other accounts you might need?"

The Case for a Payroll Account

"My last company had a payroll account," Pam said. "That did help me keep it separate."

"That's an excellent example, Pam," I said. "A separate Payroll account is another great way to get clarity on your cash situation and build some peace of mind. Allocating to another bucket to cover your in-house people rather than just burying those funds in your OpEx account is a wonderful way to track what you have to cover when payroll is due."

"That was one of the best things I ever did," Mark said. "Now I know exactly what I need to put in there for payroll each week."

"There are other great reasons to have a separate Payroll account," I said. "Many contractors still pay laborers with paper checks. Of course, each check has the routing and account numbers on it, and payroll is one of those accounts I see fraud on all of the time. If you have only one account that covers all your overhead and you get hacked or fraud occurs, it can be a serious issue. Separating payroll means that fraudsters can't drain everything in that account and leave you with no way to pay your people."

"That has happened to me twice now!" Peter declared.

"Typically, the government knows what bank account you use for payroll," I said, "because you register to pay taxes through it, so if you pay your other overhead from there—"

Knowing where I was going with this, Kevin cut me off. "Yeah, and I don't want the government in my bank account. Got in a mess with taxes years ago and the vultures cleaned me out. I barely survived it. Still gives me nightmares."

"Like someone scaring you in a dark parking lot?" I asked.

"You're never going to let me forget that, are you?" Kevin laughed.

"Anyway, those are all great reasons," I said, "but I also want you to consider this from a cash flow standpoint. Creating a separate percentage for payroll lets you know what you've been spending; if you don't have extra money in that account, for example, you know you can't afford to pay a new hire. On the other hand, your OpEx account balance can build up quickly and fool you into thinking that you do have the capacity to hire that new person. I've had many clients realize that without a clear direction on payroll, they overextend their OpEx."

Roger let out a deep breath. "Been there, done that."

"We'll cover that later when we talk about growing or contracting your business," I went on, "but if your revenue grows and your allocation percentage is consistent, a Payroll account should start building a cushion. If your revenue declines, you'll know earlier if you have to make some hard decisions. The account becomes a natural indicator of what you can afford."

"So if we add the Payroll account, do we really need the separate Owner's Compensation account?" Pam asked. "Can't we just keep up with it on spreadsheets?"

"I get that question all the time. The short answer is yes, you do need to separate it, but I'll let Roger answer this one. Roger, do you see the need for the separate Owner's Compensation account?"

"Well, I haven't missed a check since we implemented this system," he replied.

"And if your pay was tracked on a spreadsheet or on paper, what do you think would happen?" I asked.

"It would disappear. Now that you say that I agree with you—we have to have it, Pam," Roger said.

"There may be other reasons you'd want to add specific bank accounts," I said. "We talked about an account for capital expenditures, "CapEx" for short, and possibly a separate account for repairs and maintenance. What other reasons might you have to add accounts?"

Several seconds of silence ensued that seemed like an eternity, but I wanted them to brainstorm. Nobody volunteered anything, and they looked away as if they hadn't done their homework and were about to be called on by their fifth-grade teacher.

Planning for Growth with Dedicated Accounts

I FINALLY DECIDED TO LET them off the hook. "So do you have any goals in life or for your business?"

"One day, I would love to buy a building that I could call my own," Kevin said.

"Great answer," I said. "Maybe you have a long-term goal of buying that building or making some other expensive purchase that seems out of reach right now. Perhaps you're looking to move into a new line of construction and want to set aside funds for that. Maybe you've had your eye on some software that is a costly investment."

"That would be nice, to have funds set aside," Alex mused.

"Like the Payroll account example and the potential new hire, could you prepare by setting up a separate account?" I asked. "Having that buffer can help you grow more confidently. Roger, you told me about setting up a building fund and nothing was really in it, right?" I asked

"Exactly," came Roger's response.

"If you put 1% or 2% in there as you went, would you be more likely to set those funds aside?" I asked.

"It seems like that would take forever," Roger said, "versus me dumping money in there when I had extra. But I admit, that didn't work out. One workers' comp audit cash flow crunch and it was gone. Lately, I've seen how the Profit and Tax accounts have grown in the short time I've been doing this. It has been motivating."

"Thank you, Roger, that's another great example," I said. "'Unexpected' workers' comp audits, liabilities, or having to pay three months of premiums up front when that insurance renews can wreck your cash flow and perpetuate the chaos. Which tends to happen when you have a sudden increase in revenue. Let's say you have a big jump in labor—"

Alex cut me off. "That's a real concern. I had a project last year where our expected payroll doubled, and we had a massive workers' comp insurance bill that we didn't plan for."

"Really had to scrape to find that money, and it set us behind on everything," Roger said.

"So what can we all take from this?" I asked.

Alex jumped in. "You don't want to be caught off guard. We could put money aside, but without that extra account, it would get used for something else and we would be in the same boat. Given the expected growth from this job alone, we had better think about putting money aside for that."

"What else? When do you typically run out of money in this business?" I asked.

"These winter months kill me," Peter said.

"I know," I said. "You might consider a Drip account, as I mentioned before, to prepare for seasonality. It's a great way to manage cash flow during slow periods so you can make sure your employees are paid, stay current on note payments, and keep the lights on. Let's take a deeper dive into seasonality later. What about supply chain issues?" I asked.

"Yes!" Alex answered. "Coming out of COVID, we had major supply chain problems and prices went through the roof. Sometimes we know we need to put money aside for specific materials on a project, or because the owner wants to see exactly where the funds are going and make sure they aren't mishandled."

"Continue, Alex, you're doing great," I said.

"I did that a lot more in residential work," Alex said, "especially with custom home builds funded by the bank. We had to set up dedicated accounts for each project, which made tracking easier and kept the bank happy."

"I had a case with a Texas contractor who was sued for allegedly intermingling funds," I said. "They didn't do anything wrong, but the owner ran out of money and used it as an excuse to justify not paying my contractor. The contractor had to prove in court where the money went. They started setting up dedicated accounts for specific projects after that."

"Isn't that kind of extreme?" Alex asked.

"Usually, yes, I would agree, but laws are different depending on what state you're in, and some of them are not contractor friendly. I encourage anyone in the construction business to always familiarize yourself with the laws in the states you plan to work in before you bid a job that sounds good without knowing all the implications. When they see opportunity, contractors don't always look before they take the leap across state lines. I'm just suggesting that you contact a knowledgeable construction attorney in that state."

"Yeah, you're going to kill people like me with all of these accounts," Pam groaned.

"OK, Pam, let's address the reconciliation work," I said. "The banking and reconciliation process actually becomes simpler with Profit First, even if you have more accounts."

"How can that be?" Pam asked.

"Instead of all transactions flowing into and out of one account," I said, "where you have more to reconcile, you're simply moving money between accounts. It's usually much easier than you realize. For instance, all your income deposits go into one account, and then the transfers go out. If all payroll transactions are in one place, they go in and out cleanly. The same goes for the JobEx and OpEx accounts. It's very straightforward,"

"I guess I can see that," Pam said.

"With other accounts, like your Profit and Tax accounts, there are very few transactions—usually just quarterly or sporadic distributions," I said. "Mostly, it's money being transferred in. With your Owner's Comp account, it is simply allocating money to Owner's Comp and then transferring it to the Payroll account when you cover the owner's paycheck. That makes all of these very easy to reconcile."

"True. So far, those accounts have been simple to manage," Pam said.

"Yeah, but my accountant hates all this," Mark said.

"Why is that?" I asked, knowing the answer and having addressed the same concern many times.

"All these transfers in and out—the bank feeds just jumble them up," Mark explained.

"That's where having an accountant trained in Profit First helps," I said. "Bank feeds are great for importing transactions automatically. But relying on them too much can cause problems. For instance, a common complaint is that deposits in your Operating Expenses account are automatically coded as income in bank feeds. Transfers from your Income account to others aren't actual income or expenses, so that can create issues. Plus, bank feeds often don't match up properly. Personally, I find it harder to do job costing with bank feeds unless you're really on top of those accounts. It can create a mess if your accountant doesn't get the system, but if they do and you are proactive with posting your transfers, it's much faster and more efficient, even with more accounts."

"How does that work?" Mark asked.

"What most people don't realize is that taking a few minutes to enter your bank allocations as you do them can eliminate all of the confusion. You can easily create a template for this so that when the bank feeds import transactions, they are quickly and easily mapped to the proper place. If your accountant doesn't understand this or know how to handle it and is cleaning up your books after the fact, they will end up having to charge you more for that unnecessary cleanup."

"Yeah, I totally understand," Pam said. "I've been making these journal entries back and forth, but I didn't know what was going on at first."

"Pam, I was skeptical at first too," Alex told her. "But once I started allocating funds to separate accounts, it made tracking and managing project finances so much easier for me."

"A key to simplifying bookkeeping," I said, "is entering the bank transfers as you do them rather than relying on the bank feed. Do proper bank transfers between accounts. You can even memorize the percentages and transfer dates and just drop in the numbers. It's faster than you think. That way, you can avoid double-counting income or expenses and creating a mess."

"Thank you so much," Pam said. "I feel better now."

"Wade, I need to talk to you about bookkeeping," Mark said.

"OK, we can talk more about that. First, I want to address a few other reasons why contractors may want to create separate bank accounts."

Job Deposits

"What about job deposits?" I asked. "Do you ever get money for a job up front? What about mobilization money?"

"Yeah," Alex said. "We all need it."

"But do you ever borrow from that money to pay for other things?" I asked.

"We sometimes have to. We all do," Alex said. The contractors looked around at each other as if he had revealed a shared secret.

"I get it," I replied. "Depending on how your contract is written, you may have to use that money to buy materials. Since COVID, lead times have been extended for a lot of materials and many people have become painfully aware of supply chain issues. Even though things have improved, contractors learned to pay early for things that take a long time to get, like special order items or supplies that must be shipped. Delays like that can cause liquidated damages or late penalties and wreck an otherwise profitable job."

"You don't have to tell us that, but go on," Alex said.

"I had a contractor once who was working on a multimillion-dollar, multifamily project," I said. "It was all done, but the architect had specified a particular, newer part from China for the fire alarm system. The fire marshal wouldn't sign off on the buildings because of this one part, which was not at all functionally different from what was used just six months before; it was simply the latest model. The property management company wouldn't release the final draw of over $1.2 million to this contractor and couldn't rent the units, so everyone was losing money. They waited over six months for this part to be shipped from China. Eventually, the contractor explained to the architect that the parts were no different, but it still took another three months once the original part was approved to install it and get the sign-off. This $1.2 million was held up over $680 worth of parts."

"Yeah, I had a similar situation," Paul interjected. "We were working on a government contract, waiting on a specific type of electrical fixture that got held up overseas. The project was delayed by three months, and we were fined heavily for it. Since then, I've made sure to negotiate up-front payments specifically to cover any items we anticipate it will take a long time to get so that doesn't hold up my jobs. My clients appreciate it when I tell them that not paying in advance will probably delay their jobs' completion dates."

"Great, Paul. I think lots of people have learned a valuable lesson about the supply chain," I affirmed. "Smart contractors now demand that money up front to buy materials and lock in prices. Now that you have the money in hand, though, how can you keep from spending it if you haven't started the job yet? Also, you may very well have legal liability to refund that money if the job doesn't go forward."

"I never thought of that," Paul said.

"For these reasons, you might want a job deposits account. Often, owners only pay enough up front to buy materials. Many contractors ask me how to split up these deposits when they need to take some as income. How you handle it depends on the facts and circumstances, so each of you should consider your own situation when navigating this."

"These owners think we are the bank for them!" Mark scoffed.

"One positive thing to come out of the supply chain issues is that many contractors have learned to ask for money up front, especially on these cost-plus jobs, and they're not as shy about it. Whenever possible, stop being your client's finance company and ask for payment in advance. Sometimes it is easier to justify when you explain, like Paul did, that their job will be delayed without it because you can't order the materials."

"Can I get an amen?" Alex piped up.

"Requesting money up front definitely helps with cash flow," I said, "and if you can't float the materials, you shouldn't rely on lines of credit. Practically speaking, I know that's a big ask, and the industry is what it is, but just stop and ask yourself if you have to do things in the same way you always have.

"Coming back to the point here, if you get job deposits before you start work, you need to track them. You may want to put them aside in a separate account, especially if this comes up on a regular basis and you've got a liability until the job gets done or materials to purchase."

"I get them all the time. I've learned my lesson there," Paul added.

"I think you all get the point," I said. "You want to make sure that money doesn't disappear, and another bank account can help ensure that it's available when you need to buy those materials."

"Fair enough," Alex said.

"Thank you for talking to us about this," Pam said. "I think this will save me a lot of time. I just wish I didn't have to move all the money around so much."

"Yeah, it's a lot to juggle," Mark said. "But I think that if we stream-line it like you're suggesting, it could take a lot of the headache out of the process."

Automating Transfers for Cash Flow Control

"Could we somehow automate some of these transfers?" Paul asked. "You mentioned that was possible with some banks you've worked with. I didn't even know that was an option."

"That's one reason I like working with automated banking systems," I said. "They have options to automatically split funds to different accounts based on certain percentages. You shouldn't allocate every day just because you can automate it, though. I understand if you need to do that when you get started, but since the idea is to get out of the revolving door cycle with your bank accounts, it isn't the goal. Once you get rolling, I recommend that you allocate maybe once a week or twice a month. What we still need to discuss is the rhythm of how we pay out money—another key part of controlling cash flow in construction."

//

CHAPTER 9 END NOTES
Additional Bank Accounts for Clarity

Having multiple bank accounts can feel unnecessary or over-complicated at first, with concerns about added complexity, fees, and reconciliation work. However, separating funds into dedicated accounts actually simplifies cash management and there are many good reasons to set up extra bank accounts beyond the basics. Smaller balances in specific accounts provide clarity by showing you exactly how much money you have to spend on each category. While some banks may charge fees, negotiating or switching to a more accommodating bank can often resolve this issue. The key takeaway is that these accounts create a clear system for managing cash, which reduces financial confusion and makes business decisions easier.

Let's discuss a few of the items I brought up in this chapter:

A separate Payroll account is essential for keeping payroll expenses organized and secure. It provides clarity about what funds are available to cover employee wages, making it easier to plan for new hires and handle payroll during slower months. Additionally, separating payroll reduces risks like fraud or government holds on operating funds, ensuring that payroll obligations are met without disrupting other financial needs. This account also acts as an early warning system, highlighting when payroll cost may exceed what the business can afford.

An Owner's Compensation account ensures that business owners pay themselves consistently, even when cash flow is tight. Many think this account is unnecessary, especially if they track payments on a spreadsheet or handle them informally. However, unless the owner is the only employee, separating funds for compensation is crucial. Otherwise, owner paychecks are often delayed or skipped altogether when funds are tight. A dedicated account guarantees that the business prioritizes the owner's pay, fostering stability and financial discipline.

A job deposit liability account is often advisable if it helps you keep up-front payments set aside for materials and make sure funds aren't accidentally spent elsewhere. Figure 9 provides a sample format you can follow should you need to create an account for this situation.

Figure 9: Job Deposit Liability Ledger

Date	Job ID	Vendor	Deposit	Payments	Balance
1/4/2025	25-001 Jones Office Design Build		25,000.00		25,000.00
1/7/2025	25-001 Jones Office Design Build	White Cap		10,000.00	15,000.00
1/10/2025	25-001 Jones Office Design Build	Smith Supply		6,000.00	9,000.00
1/9/2025	25-003 Blue Sky Renovations		15,000.00		15,000.00
1/22/2025	25-003 Blue Sky Renovations	Home Depot		6,000.00	9,000.00

Other accounts can help you save for and keep on track with big goals, like buying a building or even setting aside money for retirement. You may still be wondering if it really makes sense to have all these accounts. As I mentioned, I have a total of nineteen bank accounts in my business. This keeps my spending in check and helps me achieve my goals. There is a quote we use in Profit First Professionals that has always resonated with me: "When in doubt, open an account." Obviously, there is a limit to how granular you want to get, but it is amazing what clarity this system will bring you.

CHAPTER 10

System Maintenance: Quarterly Reviews and Timely Actions

The Cash Flow Struggle Continues

IT HAD BEEN A FEW weeks since I last met with the guys, and they were well into the project by now. I had to hand it to them: Most of them had been trying to keep up with what they were learning and implement it in their businesses while simultaneously handling one of the biggest projects of their lives.

When I walked into the room, I saw that the usual RGC crowd was there—but then I was unpleasantly surprised to hear Dan's distinctively loud voice. He wasn't usually around; I wasn't sure if Roger and Alex had purposely kept him away or if it was his choice, but either way, his presence made me suspect that something was up.

Alex wanted to dive right in, so I started by asking everyone how things were going. Many shared that they were starting to get the hang of the Profit First allocations but didn't yet fully understand their cash flow. The clarity I knew would come with time just wasn't there yet.

"It's been a challenge to keep things in check," Mark said, "especially with the big projects we've taken on. I'm trying to get a better handle on my cash flow."

"That perfectly aligns with what I wanted to talk about today," I said.

"I haven't been in these meetings for several sessions now," Dan said, "but I still think all this Profit First stuff is bogus. It just seems like a bunch of extra work for nothing. Money comes in and money goes out. That's just the way it is in construction."

I glanced at Roger and could see him drilling a hole through Dan's head with his eyes.

"The system isn't going to work if you don't follow it," Pam said.

"I have bills to pay on my projects," Dan snapped back.

I froze for a moment, feeling like I was about to step into a pile of something.

Breaking the Cycle of Chaos

"YOU'RE RIGHT THAT CASH COMES in and goes out," I ventured. "Sometimes the inflow can be predicted and sometimes it can't. But the chaos of cash payments can be controlled."

"How? When money comes in, we have to send it out as quickly as we can to keep everyone happy," Dan shouted.

"I've seen how quickly cash can dry up when you're growing fast," Kevin responded. "Is that what's happening?"

"You're absolutely right, Kevin," I said, "but growth is a separate issue from controlling your cash. Having a system is one thing, but you must learn to manage its flow, not just the allocations. Today we're going to talk about things like the 10/24 rule described in *Profit First*. Sounds like it might just help stabilize things a bit for all of you."

"The 10/24 rule?" Mark asked.

"Yes, we will get to what that means," I said, "but we need to talk about cash flow rhythm first."

"I remember this from our conversation at the buffet place," Alex said.

"Right, Alex," I said. "It's quite common to have to allocate money daily when you start Profit First. But the idea is to let it accumulate for a certain period and then pay your bills on a schedule. Mike's book suggests what he calls the 10/24 rule. The idea is to allocate money on the tenth and twenty-fourth of each month and then pay your bills from the appropriate accounts."

"How can we possibly do that?" Dan protested.

"It's true that not every company can do it to start," I said, "but hear me out. Many of you pay your people weekly in construction. If we allocate every single day, though, we stay in that constant cycle of churning cash and create more work for people like Pam."

"Amen," Pam agreed.

"Which is not the point," I continued. "If we're so reactive to our money that we have to pay it out as quickly as it comes in, are we really getting better? We may have clarity on where that money is going, but are we really controlling the cycle?"

"It doesn't sound like it," Peter said.

"What if I have a subcontractor who shows up at my door," Dan said, "demanding money or he won't come to my job the next day? This doesn't work in construction!"

"Dan, there's a fine line between keeping good subs and setting expectations," I said.

"What do you mean?" Dan continued defiantly. "If I can't get these subs on the job, I can't get my job done."

"Do your materials suppliers also show up at your door to collect checks?"

"No," Dan replied, "not usually, anyway. I pay them every thirty or forty-five days, or whatever terms I work out with them, but they will cut me off if they don't get paid."

"What about the subs?" I asked. "Yes, you want to take care of them; I'm not suggesting you don't. Alex has a great group of subs here, and I know he wants to take care of them too."

"Yeah, but Dan's subs show up all the time expecting immediate payment." Roger shook his head. "These guys don't, as long as they get paid when their invoices are due."

"It happens almost every week," Pam sighed. Dan glared at her.

"I get what Dan's saying," Elvis said. "My guys are always at me for payments too, but there's got to be a better way to handle it."

"You can't do anything about it if those subs are cash-reactive and never learn to run their businesses," I told them. "You can, however, set the expectation that you pay on a certain day or days of the month and that they need to get their invoices in by a certain date to be paid on time."

"These guys know—" Alex said.

"Yeah, that's exactly how Alex runs it," Pam interrupted. "He sets expectations, and they all know the rules."

"What's the old saying?" Alex asked. "If you do what you've always done, you'll get what you've always gotten."

Setting a Rhythm for Payments

"THE POINT OF ALL THIS is to set a rhythm," I said. "There will be exceptions, but they should be rare. You need to set clear expectations for when invoices are due and when subs get paid. That will cut down on chaos and prevents the need to manually cut and deliver checks."

"And stress me out," Pam added.

"You need to bring structure to your cash flow," I said. "Remember, you agreed to take your profit first—if you don't, it won't be there. You need to apply that same principle of order to your construction payables and set clear guidelines."

"What did I do that was so wrong?" Dan demanded.

That's when I learned that Dan had apparently run short on a job and, with signature authority on the bank accounts, had taken money out of the Profit and Tax accounts to pay some of his materials suppliers and vendors without telling Roger. There had been a big blow-up about it at RGC.

"You mentioned this during our discussion about temptation at Megan's restaurant," Alex said, looking at me. "We had our Profit and Tax accounts in the same bank as the other accounts. You suggested moving them to another bank to ensure that they aren't raided."

"If you've got chocolate chip cookies in the house, they will get eaten," I said. "The temptation is too strong."

"They were *my* cookies, Dan," Roger said, glaring at his son.

I felt the tension getting out of hand and quickly jumped back in. "When you think about rhythm," I said, "I want you to realize that you need to get out of the cycle of letting money go out as fast as it comes in. When you draw your profit and tax first, you take the important steps of, number one, rewarding yourself for being in business and, number two, making sure that money for taxes is there when you need it. If you don't control the cycle, you will be more likely to raid those accounts for other purposes. It is essential to establish a regular, controlled flow to paying out profit and tax—a system that lets you reap the rewards of your work and update and refine your processes on a regular basis."

"Great, thanks, Wade. Why don't we take a short break," Alex said.

It was smart of him to keep more of RGC's drama from flowing out in front of the subs. Clearly wanting to avoid getting in the middle of it, a few of them had walked to the back of the room and were talking in low voices.

After a few minutes, Alex continued the meeting with the usual schedule discussion and barrage of updates. Then he transitioned to a long discussion about an extended change order issue, giving everyone a welcome break from the tension between Roger and Dan.

"Wade, can we get back to what you were talking about?" Alex asked.

"Sure," I said, walking back to the front of the room. As I turned to face the crowd, I was surprised to see that Dan had slipped away while Alex was talking. I think everyone was relieved.

"By now, you all are getting to the end of your first quarter implementing Profit First," I said, "a great time to evaluate how things have been going. Does anyone want to comment?"

We went around the room and most everyone shared something about their experience.

Quarterly Reflections: Learning from the Numbers

"The quarter's end is a great time to reflect on whether you ran short on any accounts during the period," I said. "If you did have a shortfall in one or more of your accounts, I want you to think about why."

"I ran short on my OpEx account," Mark said. "I'm not sure why, but I borrowed it from my JobEx account."

"It is common, when you get going, to find that you may not have set your allocation percentages correctly," I said. "Maybe there was something wrong in your initial calculations. But think about the reason you ran short. Was it something that came up unexpectedly?"

"A big repair bill and my workers' comp renewal payment hit at the same time," Mark said.

"It's good that you know what caused it," I said. "Looking at the reasons that create a need to 'borrow' from other accounts can help you anticipate expenses. Your workers' comp renewal was something you could have seen coming, right, Mark?"

"Yes, I should have," Mark said.

"Don't beat yourself up," I said. "That's not the point. The point is to think about this for next year."

"I definitely will," Mark said. "The renewal payment does happen at the same time every year, but it has always been a scramble to cover it. I like the thought of anticipating and keeping up with it."

"Great observation, Mark," I said. "You are starting to move from a reactive response to a more proactive position in your business."

"Love it," Peter said unexpectedly.

We talked about whether cash flow was getting a little better, and it was nice to hear some of the realizations the guys were having about how they handled their money.

"How about the flip side of running short on some of the accounts?" I asked.

"What do you mean?" Alex asked.

"Did any of you accumulate extra money in one of your accounts?" I asked. "If you borrowed from somewhere, did you think about where you borrowed it from?"

"I watched it slowly build, and it looks like I may actually have extra in my JobEx account," Paul answered.

"That's good," I said. "I often advise people to put extra money in that account so they avoid getting into the habit of borrowing from the next job."

"So what do you think I should do?" Paul asked.

"If you feel like you won't need it for job expenses," I said, "maybe you can shave a percentage point or two from that account going into this quarter and reallocate it to your Owner's Compensation or Profit account."

"I like the thought of that," Paul said.

"Ultimately, that's how you start finding more profit in your business," I said.

This kicked off an exchange among the group, led by Alex, about more lessons learned. It was beautiful to see the epiphanies that came from their shared experiences.

As he shared his insights, it was obvious that Alex had thought deeply about our conversations. I couldn't help but listen with pride: My star student was really beginning to blossom and master the art of construction cash flow.

As the conversation started to subside, Alex looked around and suddenly realized that I was no longer standing next to him and had stepped aside to let him take the floor.

"Wade, where did you go?" he asked.

"Well done, Alex," I said, walking back to the podium at the center of the room.

"So what's next?" he asked, rubbing his hands together.

"As I mentioned earlier," I said, "the end of the quarter is the time to look at our Profit account and do something with the money that has built up there. As a general rule of thumb, I suggest taking 50% of the profit as a reward for the owner. I usually advise leaving the other 50% in the business to reinvest in growth or pay down debt."

"I can buy some equipment," Mark said.

"Remember, if you buy equipment with it, it's not profit," I said. "The idea is to make the business healthier."

"Since when is investing in equipment wasting money?" Elvis asked.

"I see you haven't gotten over your equipment addiction," I said with a smile.

"No, but isn't reinvesting in my business making it healthier?" he asked.

"Elvis," Alex interjected, "you told us you haven't really reaped any rewards from your business. Contractors always justify that by telling themselves that someday things will be different. Shouldn't that some-day start now?"

"Beautifully said," I replied. "Retaining the money in the business is a great way to multiply the effects of cash flow. It's about building a healthy, sustainable business—you choose what to do with your profit, but don't justify purchasing another piece of equipment with it just to avoid pay-ing taxes. In this case, you have actual profit in cash, not just on paper."

"That's true," Elvis agreed. "Guess I need some deprogramming."

The whole group laughed.

"The end of the quarter is also a great time to revisit recurring expenses," I said. "Have more payments crept in? Can you cut some subscriptions you aren't using anymore?"

"There might be," Peter replied. "I have a subscription coming up for renewal this month that I've been meaning to cancel."

"That's precisely what I'm talking about," I said. "Sometimes we can't make all of these cuts at the same time. If you have goals for the year, this is a great time to revisit your targets and see what you can do to hit those numbers. Maybe you can find a few more percentage points to add to profit, owner's compensation, or tax until you get where you want to be."

"I'm still a long way from the profitability I think I should have," Mark said.

"That's OK," I said. "It often takes several quarters to get where we want to be. Shift a few percentage points every quarter and you'll set yourself up for long-term success."

"I've got a sixteen-year-old who has her eye on going to college out of state," Paul said. "That's going to be expensive."

"More motivation to build that healthy business," I said. "This is also a great time to reevaluate your debt. Revisit that debt schedule we did and evaluate whether your debt snowball is working. If you created Drip accounts, it's a great time to review all of them as well."

"I have knocked my debt down nicely," Mark said with a smile. "I'm proud to report that I cut more than twenty thousand dollars off my debt during this quarter. I hadn't made a dent in that debt in years, and now I'm motivated to do more."

"Staying on top of your cash can also be a good indication of whether you'll have some profit to cover before the end of the year," I said. "Using the Profit First system, you will start to see patterns develop in your cash flow as the weeks and months go by. You'll be better able to predict it over time too.

"As you approach the end of the year, it may be time to reevaluate whether you need to set aside more for taxes. If your tax allocation percentage is close to what it needs to be, you shouldn't have to scramble every April 15 to find money to pay your taxes."

"You had to spoil the fun by bringing up taxes, didn't you?" Roger joked.

"Yep," I said. "And perhaps this is the time to consider building wealth. You can tell your CPA that you don't want to buy another truck to save on taxes if you have to continue to pay for it long after you've written it off. If you buy a truck, make it a conscious decision."

"What about going into next year and looking forward?" Alex asked.

"I love where you're going with that," I said. "After the end of the year, your taxes should be covered. And you will find that you have a better handle on how you did—even before you see your CPA—than ever before because you can actually see it in your bank accounts."

"Anything else you would do at the end of the year?" Alex asked.

"Yes, but can we revisit that another day?" I asked.

"No problem," Alex said.

"I thought that Profit First would be setting and forgetting the numbers," Kevin said.

The Profit First Adjustment Process

"PROFIT FIRST IS NOT MEANT to be static," I said, "and we need to adjust our percentages over time. COVID, swings in the economy, interest rates bouncing up and down—all of these things can affect your margins. Perhaps you hired someone new or moved to a bigger office and the rent went up considerably. This is a great time to consider what effect it will have on your cash flow."

"That gives me a lot to think about," Alex said.

"We still have more to cover, and I know some of you need to get to the jobsite, but for our next discussion, I want you to start thinking about what happens to your company when it grows. What happens when the economy declines or if you lose a major contract or customer?"

///

CHAPTER 10 END NOTES
Controlling the Chaos of Construction Payment Cycles

Controlling the rhythm and timing of cash flow is essential to creating stability in a construction business. In this industry, cash often flows in and out quickly, creating chaos and stress. Subcontractors might show up demanding immediate payment, and unexpected costs like equipment repairs and insurance renewals can drain cash reserves. Not having a system in place can lead to poor decisions and leave little room to plan for the future.

To break this cycle, it's important to set a structured rhythm for managing cash flow. This means establishing regular intervals for allocating and paying money rather than doing it daily or whenever cash comes in. Creating a schedule, including specific days for payments and allocations, reduces the stress of constant demands and helps you gain clarity on your financial position. Setting clear expectations with subcontractors and suppliers is also crucial. Letting them know when invoices are due and when payments will be made helps eliminate surprises and ensure smoother operations. With a controlled cash flow rhythm, construction businesses can move from a reactive state to a proactive position, leading to better financial decision-making and sustainable profitability.

The end of a quarter—not before—is the right time to take profit. Waiting until the quarter's end protects the integrity of the system and ensures that the profit is truly available. At that point, the standard approach is to take half of the profit as a reward for the owner and leave the other half in the business. For example, I set up a "Vault" account and transfer my excess profit to it to use for a rainy day. This keeps the business healthy, whether the money is used to pay down debt or strengthen cash reserves (instead of being spent impulsively).

Quarterly reviews are an opportunity to reflect on how well your system worked. If an account ran short, take time to understand why. Was the shortfall caused by something unexpected, or something you could have anticipated like a recurring expense? On the other hand, an account surplus is a sign that adjustments might be needed. For example, you could lower the percentage going into that account and redirect it toward your Profit or Owner's Compensation account. Such adjustments help fine-tune the system, making it stronger and better tailored to your business needs.

In addition to distributing profits and reviewing accounts, a quarterly expense audit is essential. Look at all of your recurring payments to see if any can be eliminated. Subscriptions or services that no longer provide value can free up cash for other priorities.

Quarterly reviews are about celebrating wins and making small adjustments to stay on track. Later, we will dive into annual planning, where bigger changes and proactive adjustments help the system evolve with your business. For now, the focus is on staying consistent and building good habits that lead to long-term success.

As a guide, here is an abbreviated checklist to remind you what to do at the end of each quarter.

Quarter-End Quick Review Checklist

1. **Take Profits**: Distribute 50% to the owner as a reward and retain 50%.

2. **Review Accounts**: Check for shortfalls and surpluses, and adjust allocations.

3. **Celebrate Wins**: Reflect on progress.

4. **Audit Expenses**: Cut unused subscriptions and unnecessary expenses.

5. **Refine Plans**: Adjust targets and prep for next quarter.

6. **Evaluate Debt**: Track debt reduction and update Drip accounts.

7. **Plan Ahead**: Set goals for annual adjustments.

PART 4

REINFORCING PATTERNS FOR RESILIENCE AND STRATEGIC GROWTH

CHAPTER 11
Anticipating Seasonality: Planning for Predictable Cycles

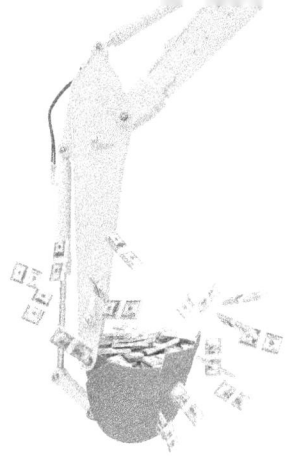

Weather Woes and Work Delays

As I WALKED INTO THE conference room one Monday morning a few weeks later, I could feel the tension in the room. It was different from last time with Roger and Dan; today everyone seemed to be in a foul mood.

The rain had been relentless over the past couple weeks, causing work to fall behind. Many of the contractors who worked outdoors couldn't make any progress on the school project. Since the building wasn't fully dried in yet, everybody was stuck, and the project was falling behind. I was glad that Alex had clued me in ahead of time; I had to walk into this one carefully.

"Should I ask how things are going?" I began cautiously as I started the meeting.

"Great, if you're a pig that likes rolling around in the mud," Elvis said. "Mud is everywhere, and it's making extra work for us."

"You guys need to get some gravel down. We've been dragging the materials through the mud for weeks," Kevin growled.

That started a flood of grumbling from the others about the impact on their billings and how the weather had turned what should have been productive weeks into wasted time that was already at a premium.

"Look, this is just part of the job," Alex said, standing up to address the group. "We all know how this works. We should count ourselves lucky that we've got work now—come next January, we may be sitting around twiddling our thumbs with nothing to bill."

A glum silence came over the room. I didn't dare speak

"Maybe we should start thinking ahead," Alex said in a positive tone. "What can we do now to prepare for those lean months?"

His words shifted the conversation from complaints to solutions, a testament to his natural leadership ability.

"Exactly what I wanted to discuss today: seasonality and how to handle its effects on cash flow," I said. "You'll be happy to know that you can do something about this."

"Uh-huh," Elvis said in his characteristic tone. "I've lived through this many times. It will be good to tell the Colonel it's fixable."

This lightened the mood a little more. Apparently, referring to his wife as "the Colonel" was a running joke with this crew.

Understanding Seasonality in Construction

"I'm not just talking about temporary, weather-related delays like rain," I continued, "but the broader changes when the seasons shift, making it too hot or too cold to work."

"I can't pour concrete when it gets too cold or rainy like this, guys," Mark said.

"We know it isn't your fault," Alex said.

"And in the Southwest, it can get so hot that roofing contractors can't even get on roofs," I said. "Not all seasonality issues are weather-related, but the thing is, most contractors face some sort of seasonal impact on their cash flow. The key is to recognize the natural ups and downs. Only then can we work on managing their impact."

"Wade, this is usually our busiest time," Alex said. "We've got a tight window to get the school done before the kids come back, so staying on schedule is critical. These delays are setting us back more than usual. We need to figure out how to make up for lost time now instead of waiting for the weather to dry out."

His focus on fixing things and finding solutions, even in challenging situations, was exactly what the team needed. When he said that, others started to open up.

"Yeah, I've got to keep my crew busy and paid. I can't have them jump ship," Kevin said. "Good people are hard to find; I can't afford to keep them, but I can't afford to lose them either."

"I completely understand," I said. "Seasonality is a natural part of many industries, and it hits different trades in different ways. There are always peak and off-peak seasons. We're not talking about economic ups and downs; that's a topic for another day. Factors like weather, client payment patterns, and economic conditions all affect our cash flow. Some are short-term, and others you may be able to see coming. That's what I'm talking about with seasonality."

"Like us killing ourselves to get school renovation projects done in the summer when the kids are out," Alex said.

"Yep," I said. "Many school boards have budgets tied to their fiscal year, which affects how and when they spend money. County governments sometimes have budgets that start in the middle of the year and must be spent by the end of their fiscal year. Other times, they run out of money and may not be able to spend until their next year's budget starts unless it's on something like emergency maintenance."

"We have that with this school board too," Alex said. "Most of the time, we can't start a project until the next year."

"Exactly. You may have to wait to start a job because your client—whether a government, a private company, or an individual—doesn't yet have the authorization or financing to pay. It could be due to fiscal-year constraints, or because they have to wait on bank draw requests. Revenue patterns can be influenced by many factors."

"On the residential side, where I used to be," Alex said, "there's often a rush to fix up homes before the holidays, followed by a really slow period after the first of the year. Also, many people plan their moves around the school year, so there's a rush for some contractors to work on units so landlords can get them rented again as soon as possible."

"More great examples, Alex," I said. "These are temporary disruptions, but some have more significant impacts than others."

"Like when your labor pool disappears," Alex said. "The start of hunting season sometimes gets us. In residential, we had certain workers who migrated around the country to chase work and weren't necessarily available when we needed them."

"Seasonality can take many forms," I said. "And I know it's not easy to manage. For example, in my world, the accounting industry, tax season is a predictable rush. Many firms have little to do in the summer. Just like you guys, they want to keep their talent, but most of the cash flows in during the first three and a half months of the year."

"Never thought of that," Peter said.

"In construction," I continued, "many seasonal impacts on cash flow are predictable too, though you may not realize it. Of course, others are not. For instance, a roofing contractor might see a sudden spike in business after a hurricane or tornado."

"No way to predict that," Alex said.

"Nope," I said. "We could spend hours talking about all the different causes of seasonality, but what's most important is that these seasonal fluctuations don't wreck your cash flow. So today, I want to focus on how we can better manage this kind of cash flow disruption."

"Got my notepad ready," Mark said. "How do we fix it?"

"First, we need to identify the patterns in our business," I said. "When do we usually see a slowdown? When are the boom times? Once we recognize these patterns, we can start planning our cash flow around them."

I noticed some of the guys nodding and knew this was starting to sink in. Most contractors know when slowdowns are coming but don't do anything to prepare for them.

Building a Financial Buffer for Slow Seasons

"Next," I continued, "we have to make sure we build up a cash reserve during the busy times. This will help carry us through the leaner months. It's not just about surviving the slow periods; it's about thriving when others are struggling."

"That's exactly right," Alex affirmed. "It's not just about getting through the tough times, it's about being able to take advantage of opportunities. If we're smart about managing our cash flow, we'll be ready to pounce on them when they come up."

"True," I said. "Look, guys, I know it's easier said than done, but if you can get ahead of the game by planning for slow periods, you can avoid a lot of stress and keep your business steady. Let's talk about some specific strategies you can use to manage cash flow better and ensure that you're ready for whatever comes your way."

"I'm listening," Kevin said.

Spotting Seasonal Cash Flow Patterns

"Alex and I sat down with Roger and Pam recently to go over RGC's cash flow," I said. "To identify the seasonality patterns in his business, we started by pulling out the last five years of bank statements."

"Five years?" Elvis asked.

"Elvis, this was eye-opening for me," Alex said.

"You probably already know the tough months," I said, "but I told him we should put it on paper. Alex, tell them how we did it."

"We spread the statements out on the table," Alex said, "and put the deposits and disbursements from the top of each bank statement into a simple spreadsheet."

"In your words, what did that accomplish?" I asked.

"We started to spot patterns," Alex said, "times when a lot of revenue came in, like in summer when school was out and construction was full speed ahead, and times when it all slowed down. A few times I also saw how we took big hits in cash that I hadn't seen coming."

"Give them some examples," I said.

"We saw a big drop in March, when there normally isn't a lot going on," Alex said. "It happened every year. Our workers' comp renewal bill hits right at that time every year too."

"What else did you see?" I asked.

"Well, the dips in March were a few months before we started to see spikes from the school billings," Alex said. "Then we had unexpected increases in equipment maintenance expenses at various times. There were many examples like that."

"Did you learn anything?" I asked. "This exercise wasn't rocket science, was it?"

"No, it was actually pretty easy to do and really illuminating," Alex said. "Roger and I actually spent a whole Saturday going back through it later."

"I didn't know you did that," I said.

"Yeah, these were things I had in the back of my mind but had never really looked at from a cash flow perspective," Alex admitted.

"Recognizing those patterns is a crucial first step," I said. "What did you do with the information?"

"We created a spreadsheet of what we noticed and need to do something about," Alex said.

"Great examples," I said. "How do the rest of you handle it in your businesses?"

Elvis mentioned getting great deals on equipment in the off-season when other contractors were dumping it because they couldn't afford the payments. Others talked about busy times with HVAC at the beginning of summer and winter. There was a discussion about frozen pipes and how plumbers got extra calls during cold spells.

It was a good discussion, and everyone agreed that they needed to go back and do the exercise with the bank statements. As we wrapped up, the conversation turned to ways to mitigate the ups and downs.

"I get that we need to build a reserve to cover expenses during slow times," Alex said. "I just keep racking my brain to come up with other work we can do when they hit."

"OK, let's go there," I said. "What are some ways you can offer more stable employment for your people? Let's talk about expanding into other services or doing work that isn't weather-dependent."

"I've been thinking about branching into some small-scale renovations," Mark said. "It's not as glamorous, but it could keep the guys busy when the weather's bad."

"Diversifying services is one approach," I said. "Kevin has a different kind of challenge. He's grown his mechanical contracting business rapidly, but that growth has brought cash flow issues of its own."

"It's like I'm always chasing my tail," Kevin said. "We've been looking at how to smooth out those rough patches by tightening up on receivables during the busy times and renegotiating payment terms with suppliers when things slow down. I've started calling some clients to nudge them a bit on overdue invoices. It's not fun, but it's making a difference."

"Good proactive approach," I said. "Peter, what about your plumbing business?"

"My business was passed down from my father," Peter said. "We are struggling with inventory management and credit lines with supply houses. We have trouble keeping people and our cash flow never seems to improve. We stocked up on some things during COVID because we couldn't always get the materials we needed, and that has put us in a cash spiral."

He talked about the self-help business books he'd read, trying to find a magic bullet that would fix his business. Seasonality compounded his existing challenges.

Paul brought up skyrocketing materials prices and labor costs. He was deep in debt despite having strong receivables. His seasonality issues were less about time and more about market conditions that tended to shift without warning.

We also discussed looking at credit balances to see if they went up at a particular time of year, and how when you pay them down can be a key indicator of seasonality. (Running up credit cards signifies a cash flow deficit too.)

"So we all agree that certain times of year are better than others, right?" I asked.

"Right," Alex said for the group.

"We talked previously about how to create Drip accounts," I said, "and set aside funds specifically for those unexpected swings. You may also need to set aside funds for the ones you can see coming."

"Agreed," Alex said. "So how do we figure that?"

"After recognizing that you have a problem," I said, "you need to evaluate the amount you need to cover the shortfall. The idea is to predict the challenge, prepare for it, and smooth out your cash flow."

"Is it as easy as looking at last year, evaluating what might be different this year, and shooting for saving that amount?" Alex asked.

"Pretty much," I said. "Again, you may not cover the entire shortfall, especially in the first year, but you can lessen the impact. After that it gets easier."

"The key is getting started, got it," Alex said.

//

CHAPTER 11 END NOTES
Evaluating Your Seasonality Profile
and Recognizing Seasonality in Construction

"SEASONALITY" REFERS TO PREDICTABLE PATTERNS of work slowing down or picking up due to external factors. It is a natural part of many industries, and construction is no exception. Weather often plays a major role—rain, snow, and extreme temperatures can delay projects and reduce productivity. In colder climates, pouring concrete might be impossible during the winter months, while in hotter regions, roofing can be dangerous during peak summer heat. Beyond weather, seasonality can also be driven by client schedules. For example, school construction often ramps up in the summer when students are on break, while residential contractors often see a rush before the holidays as homeowners tackle last-minute projects.

Identifying these patterns starts with looking at your own business history. Review financial records from the past several years to spot trends. When do you typically see the most revenue? When are expenses at their peak? You might notice, for example, that a big insurance payment is always due the same month or that equipment maintenance spikes in a certain season.

Figure 11, below, provides a template for reviewing seasonality in your business. This exercise can be useful in anticipating ups and downs in cash flow and helping you better prepare for them. A few things to note:

1. The template I have provided spans one year, but ideally, I suggest you look at up to five years' worth of both deposits and expenses.
2. When extracting numbers from your bank statements:
   a. Subtract any transfers in and out of the accounts or loans from the owner and only include income deposits in your analysis.
   b. Also subtract any transfers to other bank accounts from your disbursements, and subtract any personal disbursements for the owners, such as taxes that might need to be paid.
3. After listing these, divide the total deposits for the month by the total deposits for the year. Do the same with expenditures. This will provide percentages that show spikes in your revenue and expenses.
4. If you do undertake an analysis of more than one year and can put the information in a spreadsheet like Excel, it is often useful

to put the year's deposits and expenses side by side to uncover patterns. Excel is also great for creating line graphs that show spikes or dips in income or expenses.

Figure 11: Seasonality Profile

Revenue Profile	Year 1 $	Year 1 %	Expense Profile	Year 1 $	Year 1 %
January	$	%	January	$	%
February		%	February		%
March		%	March		%
April		%	April		%
May		%	May		%
June		%	June		%
July		%	July		%
August		%	August		%
September		%	September		%
October		%	October		%
November		%	November		%
December		%	December		%
Total Revenue	$	100%	Total Expenses	$	100%

If you spot a seasonality issue in your business that you want to mitigate, create another bank account to address it and drip funds into that account throughout the year. See the equipment Drip account exercise in Chapter 7 for a template you can use to get started.

CHAPTER 12
Managing Curveballs: Navigating Cash Flow Disruptions

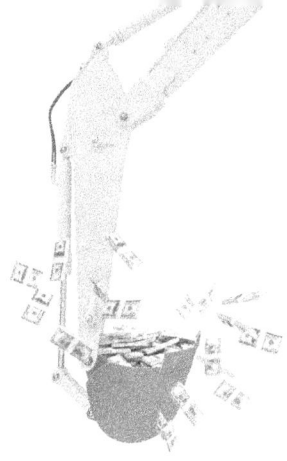

Weathering the Storm

A FEW WEEKS WENT BY, and the weather turned for the better. The rain stopped and it started to warm up. I hoped that meant things had gotten better for everyone.

Walking through the dimly lit parking lot for the next meeting, I could see Mark's large frame approaching. He was the type of big man who could be a bit intimidating at first, the kind of guy you'd love to have in your corner if you were going out to chase payments on receivables, but he was also a total teddy bear once you got to know him. As we closed the distance between us, I saw that he had a big grin on his face.

"Good morning," Mark said. "You called it!"

"Called what?" I asked.

Facing Cash Flow Shortfalls

"THAT WE MIGHT RUN SHORT in some of our accounts," he said. "The slowdown on the job meant I didn't have enough to cover some expenses and had to take money from my Profit and Tax accounts. I paid it back already, but for future reference, what do I do in this situation?"

"Perfect, let's talk about that today," I said.

Everyone was standing around drinking coffee when we walked in. Alex and most of the crew had gotten there early this time.

"Am I late?" I asked.

"Not at all. Everyone was just eager to get the job updates out of the way," Alex said. "We're ready to jump in if you are."

"Sounds good," I said. "How are you all holding up?"

"Last month was rough," Mark said. "We kept our crews busy trying to catch up, but cash didn't come in because of low pay apps from the month before. We still had to pay that labor."

"Yeah, and we got hit with that workers' comp renewal we talked about last time," Alex added. "More money out of pocket that we hadn't planned on. We'll be prepared for it next year, but that doesn't help us with the last few weeks."

The floodgates opened.

The Unexpected Hits Hard

"I HAD A TRACK GO out on my excavator," Elvis said. "I knew I needed to pay attention to it, but I didn't have the time or money to fix it. I was forced to fix it because I have to have it working on the job. Am I in trouble with the principal? What's the plan? How do I fix it?"

"I totally understand. And look, delays and unexpected expenses are a fact of life," I said. "Unfortunately, construction is unpredictable. There are no rules here that are written in stone, but I want to give you some guidelines."

"Before you do, we have another problem," Alex said. "We got hit with some legal bills from one of Dan's jobs. He didn't handle the electrical work right. Roger was doubting the whole system and wondering if we should scrap it."

Before I could respond, Dan spoke up from the back of the room. I hadn't seen him yet because he was sitting alone in a corner. Now he tried to defend himself.

"I get it," Dan said. "I messed up on that job, but it wasn't entirely my fault. The plans were a mess, and I wasn't given all the information I needed. I'm doing everything I can to make it right, but those legal bills weren't just because of my work."

Now it was Paul's turn. "The cost of my materials has gone through the roof," he said. "I've been trying to keep us under budget, but when suppliers keep jacking up prices, it's a losing battle. Anyway, I had a bunch of bills hit and we didn't get much money in this month. My suppliers were going to withhold a shipment."

"OK, everybody," I said. "I know the timing of bills can suck. Unexpected expenses will come up, no matter how well you prepare. The key is to not let it wreck your system."

"I told you this stuff doesn't work," Dan said snidely.

"Guys, trust me," I said, trying not to let Dan annoy me, "as the weeks and months go by, it gets easier. Your allocations won't be perfect at first, but you will refine them as you go. Even if you get your allocation percentages right from the start, you need guidelines to keep you from throwing the baby out with the bathwater until you build up your reserves."

"So what should we do?" Mark asked. "What should I have done?"

"We've already talked about setting up bank accounts for unexpected expenses and slowdowns. You can call it a rainy-day fund, a Drip account, a Vault account, whatever you want. You might take some of your quarterly profit and set it aside in an account like this. That's not what this is about."

"Then what *is* it about?" Dan said loudly.

The Danger of Wrecking the System

"It's about not wrecking your system as soon as things go wrong," I said. "I have been helping contractors implement Profit First for many years now. They get stuck in this analysis paralysis about getting started. They think the process sounds doable, but they never get off the ground because they don't understand how to set up the bank accounts, do their assessment, or allocate funds. Even if they do get started, situations like these come up and they quit before they see what it's like on the other side."

"So tell us what it looks like, Wade," Alex said.

"Total transformation in the lives of my contractors," I said.

"That's why I'm here," Mark said. "Preach!"

"If I sound like I'm preaching, I apologize," I said. "It's just that it's heartbreaking for me to see contractors bail on Profit First when something goes wrong. Unfortunately, I've seen it more times than I want to admit—a challenge comes up, the system is derailed, and they go back to doing it the old way that never led them to profitability in the first place."

"Why do you care?" Dan said.

"Again, I have seen the other side of this," I said. "I saw the turnaround in my own firm first, and subsequently I've been privileged to see it with my contractors as they finally find the success they are looking for. Dan, *that's why I'm here.*"

A short silence came over the room.

"So, Mark, how did you handle your shortfall?" I asked.

"Yeah, like I told you, I had to raid my Profit and Tax accounts to cover it," Mark admitted.

"And Elvis? What did you do?" I asked.

"I had to pull money from my own pocket because I didn't want to be the weak link in the group," Elvis said, slightly embarrassed. "What else could I do? What should I have done?"

"I understand, and both of you did what you needed to do," I said. "Nobody is in trouble with the Profit First police here. As for how to handle it, the first step is to assess whether the expense is temporary or ongoing. Mark, having at least that in reserves helped, right?"

"It was definitely good that I had it to use," Mark said. "I'm glad I did because otherwise, I would've had to take out one of those pay-by-the-week loans that cost so much in interest. Those people are vultures! I can't believe what they can get away with. Anyway, in the past, it wouldn't have been there."

"Exactly," I said. "It does get easier. Borrowing from company accounts is tricky, though. You can say you'll pay back the money, but often that doesn't happen, especially in a tight cash flow situation. If you can, taking it out of your own pocket like Elvis did is better—but it isn't ideal either."

"I'm going to pay myself back," Elvis said. "The Colonel will make sure of that."

"Exactly. You're more likely to pay back funds that came out of your own pocket," I said. "When you borrow from one account to shore up another, it's easy to justify and forget. You shouldn't have to take it from your own pocket either; you feel the pain there too. The key is, if we keep borrowing from ourselves or our Profit and Tax accounts, that cash profit we were working toward disappears just as magically as it did before we tried this."

"So how do we know what to do?" Alex asked.

"Look, what Mark and Elvis did was exactly what needed to be done in the moment," I said, "but let's break it down so you're all ready for next time. Before you do anything else, pause and evaluate the situation. Ask yourself: Is this a one-time expense or something that could recur in the future? Is it something we can plan for? Anticipating these issues is half the battle."

"Then it isn't so unexpected," Alex said.

"Right," I said. "Mark, you've had your share of unexpected expenses, and I know you are working on building those reserves. Remember, it's not just about solving today's problem but also ensuring that you're not blindsided tomorrow. Set up that liability account and be disciplined about paying yourself back too."

"Gotcha," Mark replied.

"Elvis, you've dealt with cash flow challenges too," I said. "Here's the key: you've got to be proactive, not reactive. If we protect our Profit, Owner's Comp, and Tax accounts first, we're in a much stronger position. It's about strategy, not just surviving from day to day."

"Lesson learned," Elvis said. "I know this will get better."

"It will," I said. "Folks, if you need to cover operating expenses or something unexpected and have nowhere else to pull from, you might have to borrow from your JobEx account. But remember, that's money you'll have to make up later, assuming that your JobEx percentages are set up correctly. Sometimes, I purposely allocate an extra percentage point to JobEx at the start to build a buffer and break the cycle of borrowing from the next job."

Building Reserves for the Future

"I SEE HOW THAT COULD help with our growth," Alex said.

"Yes," I said, "and we will talk about that too. The side benefit is that it can help with unexpected expenses and reduces your reliance on lines of credit that you will have to pay back later, with interest. If the balance in your JobEx account grows consistently and you don't need all of it, it might be time to reevaluate your allocation percentages. You might see the same with your OpEx account. We'll discuss when it's the right time to reassess."

"I can put those extra percentage points toward profit next quarter," Alex said.

"That's the idea," I said. "As a company's revenue grows—and we'll talk about growth another day—operating expenses will probably increase. If your other accounts start building healthy balances, you can draw from them first if you have to. Guys, again, there are no hard and fast rules here, but strategies like these can help you avoid repeating old cycles."

"I just wish I had a bigger line of credit for when something like this happens," Kevin said.

"Creating reserves and strengthening your balance sheet is a great way to build your credit rating. If you don't have a line of credit, a healthy financial statement can go a long way toward establishing one and helping to maintain a good relationship with your bank."

"I got in trouble with running up a line of credit years ago," Paul said.

"It's easy to do," I said, "especially for a contractor who hasn't been taking a regular paycheck. There's a balance between growing your business and maintaining financial health."

"So Mark's not in trouble?" Alex joked.

"Not at all," I said. "There's nothing inherently wrong with what Mark, Elvis, or anybody else did to get through tough times. These things happen, especially when you're getting used to Profit First. The key is to stick with the system and remember the fundamentals."

"You don't have to answer to my wife," Mark joked.

///

CHAPTER 12 END NOTES

Managing Curveballs: Preparing for the Unexpected

UNEXPECTED EXPENSES ARE A NORMAL part of running a construction business. No matter how much you plan, things like equipment repairs, rising materials costs, and surprise bills can catch you off guard. These moments can feel overwhelming, but they don't have to derail your Profit First system.

The goal is to handle shortfalls without breaking the structure you've worked hard to build. By preparing for emergencies with a rainy-day fund, you can cover unexpected costs while protecting your Profit and Tax accounts. It's not always easy at first, but sticking to the system helps you stay in control and your business moving forward in spite of the surprises.

Inevitably, things will happen, and you will have to cover gaps based on your own situation. My goal is to give you a framework to follow when something like this occurs, noting that there will be hiccups as you get started and get used to the system. Beyond that, you need to start by asking yourself four questions about why the shortfall occurred.

Questions to Ask When a Shortfall Occurs

1. Is this expense a onetime issue or a recurring problem?
2. If I could have anticipated this expense, how can I prepare for it in the future?

3. Which account can I borrow from temporarily without under-mining my long-term goals?

4. How will I rebuild reserves and strengthen my system to avoid this in the future?

Framework for Handling Cash Shortfalls in the Profit First System

1. **Pause and Evaluate**

   a. Identify the Cause: Determine whether the expense was unex-pected or could have been anticipated. Assess whether it is a onetime issue or a recurring problem.

   b. Assess Timing: Evaluate whether delayed payments or other timing issues contributed to the shortfall.

   c. Reflect on Preparedness: Consider whether reserves or buffers were available to help.

2. **Categorize the Expense**

   a. Onetime Expense: Examples include equipment repairs, sur-prise legal bills, and temporary cost increases. Use emergency reserves or temporarily borrow from Profit or Tax accounts.

   b. Recurring or Systemic Problem: Examples include consistently high materials costs and underfunded operating expenses. Reassess allocation percentages or adjust pricing.

3. **Handle the Shortfall Strategically**

   a. Use Reserves First: Tap into a rainy-day fund or buffer account, if available.

   b. Borrow if Necessary: Use Profit and Tax accounts as a last resort and create a repayment plan.

    c. Avoid Outside Debt: If possible, minimize reliance on high-interest loans or credit lines.

4. Develop a Recovery Plan

    a. Rebuild Reserves: Allocate funds in the next quarter to replenish accounts.

    b. Adjust Percentages: Refine allocation percentages if certain accounts are regularly underfunded.

    c. Set New Habits: Plan for similar expenses in the future by building them into JobEx or OpEx allocations.

5. Learn and Improve

    a. Analyze Patterns: Identify trends in shortfalls.

    b. Plan for Predictable Cycles: Reserve funds for seasonal slowdowns, large annual payments, and similar predictable costs.

    c. Strengthen Financial Discipline: Maintain adherence to the Profit First system to prevent reversion to old habits.

CHAPTER 13

Building Resilience: Cash Flow Management in Uncertain Times

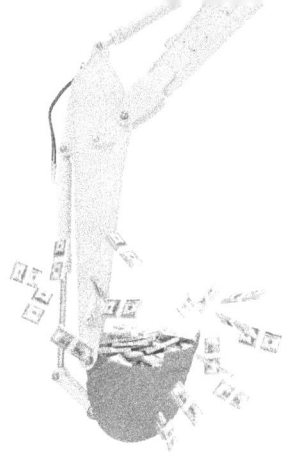

Learning from the Past: Economic Cycles and Construction

As we wrapped up the discussion about unexpected expenses, I noticed Roger slip in quietly.

"Welcome, Roger," I said.

"Sorry I'm late," he said. "I had another meeting, but I was hoping you have a solution for the cash crunch we went through. Did you tell him about it, Alex?"

"Yes," Alex replied. "I know how to handle it next time."

"That's great," Roger said. "At least we're not back in the aftermath of the 2008 meltdown."

"Yeah, that totally sucked," Elvis said. "The folks who've been in this industry for a while all took some hard knocks from that. The younger crowd can't appreciate what we went through."

"Good point," I said, "but there are some important lessons we can all draw from that time. First, you all know that economic cycles come and go and are constantly evolving. There will always be ups and downs. Construction is often hit harder than other industries."

"You don't have to tell me," Roger said, "I've lived through a few downturns."

"True, they aren't unusual," I said, "but the one after 2008 was particularly rough because of its severity and the length of time it took to recover. COVID also had some extreme effects on the industry, depending on where you were in the country and the type of work you do. Some contractors actually did better and grew during that time, while others would have been totally devastated by it had the government not provided disaster loans and assistance."

"That saved my butt," Mark replied.

"Back to the topic at hand," I said. "What I want you to realize is that these extremes make clearer what actually happens constantly in the construction industry. Roger, you brought up a good point. How should we respond during an economic downturn? How does Profit First address that?"

"I wish I knew," Roger replied.

Knowing Elvis's history, I asked, "Elvis, from your perspective, what happened in the grading and heavy equipment industry back in 2008?"

The Cost of Misplaced Confidence

"This is a sore spot for me," Elvis replied, "but I'm glad to talk about it. The company I worked for then was heavily invested in equipment, like I am now. When things started to crumble for everyone else in 2008 and 2009, we thought we were fine because we had some work. By 2010, the work dried up, the debt was too great, and they had to close forever. The owner had a lot of real estate that had been in his family for generations and lost it all."

Mark was known for liking the finer things in life. He was a spender, so I wanted his take on this.

"Mark, what happened to you during the Great Recession?" I asked.

"I'm not proud of this," Mark started, "but most of you know about it anyway. We had to close too after getting in trouble on a bonded job. We bankrupted one company, and I had a hard time finding money to support my family during that time. I drove a truck for a little while just to make ends meet. I eventually managed to pivot back to the concrete and masonry business by focusing on smaller projects. It took many years to get back to where I am now."

"Thanks, Mark," I said. "I didn't mean to get too personal."

"It's OK," Mark said. "I used to be embarrassed by it, but I did have to file bankruptcy. I'm only just starting to be able to bond jobs again and will probably never get the low rates we used to again. I guess I learned that no matter how much revenue you've got, if you aren't profitable, your business will ultimately crash down around you."

"There are several lessons in what you both related," I said. "Contractors had less work available, so I saw people taking jobs at lower prices just to keep their doors open. All of that extra competition led to everyone underbidding projects to try and get cash flowing and keep the doors open."

"Saw that too," Elvis said.

"Contractors of all types got caught up in a perpetual cash flow game," I said. "One vivid example I can give you was a client company that had a fleet of trucks. Every year they played the same tax game, buying another one or two just to get the tax deduction."

"Isn't coming up with deductions the job of a good CPA?" Roger asked.

"That might be expected of most CPAs," I said. "I thought it was my job too, and to some degree it still is, but the aftermath of the Great Recession changed my thinking."

"How so?" Alex asked.

The Cash Flow Illusion Trap

"By the end of 2010," I replied, "many contractors found themselves with no work, just as Elvis described. In one case, I saw a company collecting their 2010 receivables in early 2011, but they had zero work scheduled for 2011. The cash that seemed to pour in during the first few months of 2011 stopped like a cruel game of musical chairs. The comfort of having that cash in the bank was a mirage, and the continued expenses soon followed, leaving them with a mountain of debt."

"I think we can guess what happened," Alex said.

"Yes," I said, "this once thriving company's machine stopped, so they ended up laying everyone off. They had to dump all those trucks they didn't need on the market for less than they were worth. Everybody was doing the same thing, so the trucks lost a lot of value. They owed more on these vehicles than they were worth. They also had to come up with money to get rid of their equipment because they were upside down on the debt."

"Just when we were starting to feel good about this again," Kevin said.

Profit First as a Shield Against Downturns

"This is actually a good thing," I said, "and something I have thought about for years. I often wonder what it would have meant for companies like that if Profit First had been around before the Great Recession. Some of these contractors might still be in business today."

"Say more about that," Roger said.

"I will in a bit," I said. "COVID was bad, but it could have been much worse had the government not propped things up. The bigger challenge we faced coming out of the pandemic was that it left a huge hole in the supply chain. The demand for construction was high, but you couldn't get the materials you needed, driving up prices. I don't have to tell you guys that."

"These ups and downs in the economy are inevitable," Roger said. "Live long enough and you will see them come and go."

"True, but that's not the lesson here," I said. "Given that downturns are not a question of if, but when the next one will happen, we need to be ready. That's where these Profit First principles become invaluable. It's about staying ahead, not just surviving. One electrical contractor I worked with recognized some of the early warning signs. I will spare you the details, but he told me his cash was dwindling and that profits were nonexistent on available jobs. He asked me if he should shut down. I agreed that he should because his retirement was slipping away."

"Most people didn't have that luxury," Elvis said.

"No, they didn't," I said. "The point is, he relied on his cash to tell him to shut down. Remember the story I just told you about the thriving company that collected their receivables and then had no work?"

"Uh-huh," Elvis said.

"What I didn't say was that they were fooled by their cash flow," I said. "Because of the temporary influx of cash from those receivables, they thought that things would improve and held off on making the rational decision to close down."

"So what are you saying?" Alex asked.

"I'm saying that both owners made decisions based on what was in their bank accounts," I said. "One happened to be a good decision, but the other ended in disaster. These bank account-based decisions affect our thinking around both business and personal finances."

"Now I'm confused," Kevin said.

An Early Warning System

"WHAT I'M SAYING IS THAT you now have a system in place to give you early warning signs of change, good or bad," I said. "It tells you what to do in your business when cash starts running out in your Payroll account or your JobEx account suddenly runs short because materials went through the roof. Right now, we're talking about declines, but we also need to address growth."

"I can see that," Alex said.

"You would be surprised how well the system functioned for some of my contractors during the pandemic," I said. "Some had to make hard decisions because their Payroll accounts were drying up. In other cases, OpEx accounts running short signaled that overhead might need to be cut. JobEx accounts ensured that they had the money to cover existing work, but also signaled that pricing needed adjusting when they started running short."

"Wow!" Kevin said.

"So, Kevin, does this make you think about the kind of clarity you had before, with one bank account?" I asked.

"Yeah, I was even more lost. But what about when you are in growth mode?" Kevin asked.

"Let's pick that up next time," Alex said. "I've got to get out to the job now to meet an inspector."

//

CHAPTER 13 END NOTES

Building Resilience in Uncertain Times

I HOPE THAT NONE OF us ever have to deal with a downturn as severe as the Great Recession of 2008 and its aftermath again or, heaven forbid, a depression like the one that occurred in the 1930s.

The reality is that economic cycles come and go. History has shown that patterns recur, but the timing, length, and severity of downturns are all unpredictable.

Working with contractors all over the country has taught me that these cycles are not felt equally in different regions or even within different areas of the same state. Commercial projects may be nonexistent in one area while other areas are booming. Downturns in construction spending may be at the commercial or residential level, or even within individual trades. Many are mild and may not last long, but the point is that you need to be able to handle them no matter their severity.

While it is long past 2008 as I write this, that recession affected the industry significantly. I saw friends lose everything. I want you to understand the typical responses and what happens to cash flow so you can handle such crises appropriately.

I did extensive research following those years on companies that do and don't survive downturns. I won't bore you with a deep dive into that here; suffice it to say that those who are prepared can not only survive; they can also emerge as industry leaders when they come out the other side.

You will be happy to note that there is no homework for this chapter, but you may want to revisit it if this is happening to you. Here's a brief recap of what happens during a typical economic decline in construction.

What Happens During an Economic Decline

1. Work availability decreases.
   a. Fewer available projects can lead to increased competition,
   b. Which can result in contractors undercutting bids to secure cash flow,
2. Leading to cash flow struggles.
   a. Businesses experience a cash crunch as receivables dwindle,
   b. Which may lead to debt burdens becoming unsustainable and possible insolvency.
3. Emotional decision-making can take over.
   a. Construction company owners typically want to believe the best and sometimes resist making hard decisions.
   b. The natural tendency is to make decisions based on bank account balances rather than sound strategies.
   c. This can result in attempts to make short-term fixes, such as borrowing on exorbitant pay-by-the-week loans, and lead to long-term issues.
4. Decisions are made about overhead and equipment costs.
   a. Companies often carry excess overhead or unneeded equipment in hopes of recovery.
   b. If the situation lasts too long, it can lead to fire sales where depreciating equipment may lead to upside-down loans and increased financial pressure.

The Typical Responses of Construction Business Owners

1. Cash in the bank can fool the best of us, especially when we are operating with one bank account.
   a. Owners may collect dwindling receivables but have no backlog.
2. This tends to start a cycle of lowering bids and accepting lower-margin work.
   a. Lowering prices to keep cash flowing can lead to a vicious cycle that is hard to get out of.
3. After that, if insufficient cash comes in from work, owners tend to borrow because they believe that the situation is temporary.
   a. Naturally, owners want to hold onto good employees and not cut expenses.
4. Cost-cutting starts to occur when owners realize that cash still isn't coming in.
   a. This leads to reductions in the workforce, cutting overhead where possible, and dumping equipment to lower expenses
   b. This is often reactive and too late to prevent major losses or failure.

How Profit First Helps During Downturns

1. Clear financial signals become evident faster.
   a. Cash running short in accounts (e.g., JobEx or OpEx) provides early warnings that something needs to change.
   b. The bank setup clearly shows where a cash deficit is occurring.
2. Decision-making has guardrails.
   a. The systematic allocation structure encourages deliberate action instead of emotional reaction.

    b. Owners can identify financial stress early and adapt strategically.

3. Reserves create preparedness.

    a. Building rainy-day or emergency funds allows businesses to sustain operations and cover overhead and obligations during low-revenue periods.

4. The focus is on profitability.

    a. Profit First encourages contractors to maintain profitability rather than chase cash flow.

    b. This helps prevent underbidding by revealing the true cost of operations from a cash perspective.

5. Pricing is adaptable.

    a. The system highlights when pricing needs to be adjusted to reflect materials costs or cash shortages.

    b. This promotes proactive changes rather than reactive measures.

6. Owners gain long-term stability.

    a. Profit First ensures that businesses survive downturns by allowing them to maintain financial stability,

    b. Positioning companies to emerge even stronger when the economy recovers.

CHAPTER 14
Growing Wisely: Balancing Expansion with Cash Stability

The Highs and Lows of Cash Flow

It had been a few weeks since we last met, and I was eager to see how things were going. When Alex called to arrange our next meeting, I agreed to come in a little later so the crew could go over the schedule first thing.

I arrived just after gales of laughter erupted following a remark from Elvis about the Colonel, and I could tell immediately that the collective mood had changed for the better. The guys' smiles and positive attitudes had returned.

"Wade, glad you're here," Alex greeted me. "After the weather setbacks, we rallied and were able to accelerate production. We are actually a week ahead of schedule now! We sent out our biggest pay app last month and just got paid for it a few days ago."

"It's funny how having money in your bank account can change your mood," I said.

The Temptation of Extra Cash

"Yeah, it was a little depressing last time," Elvis said, "talking about what happens when things go south, but I'm really looking forward to this next draw. I've got my eye on a backhoe the salesman just got in on trade; he's going to give me a great deal on it. I really can't wait until we wrap this thing up and get that big retainage check."

Alex, who had moved to the front row to allow me to take the podium, immediately glanced at me. I knew exactly what he was thinking about: Dan buying that stupid truck before the company had put the first shovel in the ground.

Pam and Roger were both back this time too. I realized later that what you should do when you feel like you have extra money in your account had become a hot topic at RGC.

"Elvis, that sounds like Dan and the truck," Alex remarked.

"Yeah, we all know about Dan and spending money he didn't have," Elvis said. "Obviously I've got to pay my overhead, but my accounts are pretty much holding steady right now. I had a retainage check come in about a month ago from an old job, and I didn't know what to do with it all or how to handle it."

"We have finally started catching up too," Pam said with a smile. "We've enjoyed having a break from the usual cash crunch at RGC. I thought we'd stick the extra in the Profit account and let it sit. Roger usually gives us a bonus based on whatever profit is left over at the end of the year, so I wanted to make sure there was more in there."

The Danger of Going Off-Script

"Pam, how is this different from the old approach?" I asked.

"I agree," Alex said. "Wade, should we be going off-script and changing the system? Should cash move through the system differently because we've got more than we currently need?"

"That was actually my idea too, to put it aside," Roger said, "but Pam moved the money. It was just sitting there, so I thought I'd take a bonus check for myself. I figure I deserve it."

"So why didn't you use the normal allocation?" Peter asked. "Wade, what do you think?"

"You guys are doing fine, keep going," I said. "Pam?"

"Because it was such a large deposit," Pam replied. "I didn't feel like we needed all of it."

"I get wanting to take it," said Mark.

"I'm glad this came up," I said. "There's wisdom in talking this through. Alex, continue with your thoughts."

"Pam, have you fully funded the reserves?" Alex asked. "Do you have our seasonality account covered yet?"

"Well, no, but—"

Peter cut Pam off. "I did the same thing," he said, "and paid off a lot of my debt. I'm working toward that healthy business Wade was talking about."

"Peter, did you check to make sure there weren't other things that needed paying?" I asked.

"I guess I should have thought about that more," Peter admitted. "Two days later an invoice from a materials supplier showed up that I forgot about. I ran short and had to send a partial payment. I told them I would cover it with my next draw."

"Peter, I'm glad you were able to make arrangements," I said, "but it sounds like you could have ended up having to get one of those pay-by-the-week loans. Pam, what happened with that money? Is it still in the Profit account?" I asked

"About that," Roger replied. "I had to borrow some of it."

"*Borrow*?" I asked.

"Well, I've been meaning to give myself a bonus," Roger said. "I missed a lot of paychecks. Not lately, mind you, but my paychecks were sporadic for years."

"Again, there are no hard and fast rules. I do, however, want you to consider what we talked about last time," I said.

"What do you mean?" Mark asked. "Last time we were scrambling to come up with funds; now we are able to enjoy some of it. It's not the same thing."

"Well, you had to go off-script then," I said. "You are doing the exact same thing here. Now, I get it, but what you need to consider are the consequences of changing allocation percentages arbitrarily or for one large deposit."

"I see where you are going with this," Alex said. "Just like big hits to your cash flow, big influxes can cause reactive behavior."

"You mean me and that equipment," Elvis said, laughing. "I guess I need to go into equipment rehab."

"The first step is to admit you have a problem," Mark joked.

"Everybody, Elvis can do what he wants to do," I said. "The thing is that temptation is ingrained in all of us. It's how we're wired. But just like I wanted you to pause when you had to borrow money from other accounts when you ran short, I want you to pause when you have extra and are tempted to arbitrarily change your allocation percentages."

"Can you give us some rules to follow?" Alex asked.

"I can only give you general advice," I said, "and the first thing I would tell you is to allocate the money in the usual proportions. Second, Alex, do you remember the discussion about small plates versus large plates when we were at Megan's for lunch? If a balance in an account is truly more than you need, it can be tempting. Consider moving it to your rainy-day fund, your emergency fund, or wherever you need it most. Paying off debt is a great way to ensure that you don't overspend profit, but again, just make sure you don't need it for something else before you do. What do you think about that as a start, Alex?"

"I agree that consistency with the allocations, even if there's an over-abundance, is critical," Alex replied. "What do you guys think?"

"I can understand the point about temptation," Mark said. "I know we talked about when to take profit and you said at the end of the quarter, but can we talk about that more?"

"Sure," I said, "but there is one more related topic I want to get to first. Alex, you're doing great with this discussion—anything else?"

"Roger, did you figure you'd have extra profit when you bid the job?" Alex asked.

"Well, no," Roger replied.

" Pam, do you feel like you've built the reserves we need?" Alex asked.

"We have some, but not enough," Pam admitted.

"Then there's your answer," Alex concluded.

"How do I know how much of a reserve to aim for?" Pam asked.

"I often help my clients set a goal related to what it takes to run their business. Perhaps you want two, three, or even four months' worth of overhead in the bank. That can give you a strong sense of security."

"OK, I like that," Pam said. "I will kick that around with Roger. Thanks."

"All right, can we change direction now?" I asked. "I want to talk about what happens to cash flow during a growth phase. Kevin, we talked briefly about your growth last time, but you haven't said anything yet today."

Growth Doesn't Always Mean Profit

"About that," Kevin said. "I'm embarrassed to admit that I must be doing something wrong."

"Why do you say that?" I asked.

"Because I have the opposite problem," he said. "Sure, plenty of money is coming in, but I can't seem to keep any of it. I thought things would smooth out as I added to my top line revenue, but it's actually been the opposite; I've been even more strapped for cash."

"Kevin, that doesn't make sense," Alex said. "Wade, how can that be?"

"This is what I refer to as the 'Construction Growth/Profit Paradox,'" I said.

"The *whut*?" Elvis said.

"Maybe I will write a book about it one day," I said. "We can't take a deep dive into it now, but it does play into what I wanted to discuss today. Kevin, let me ask you a few questions to see if I am right."

"OK, shoot," Kevin said.

"You say you have been growing rapidly, right," I said. "Do you mind sharing your top line revenue numbers? What does growth look like for you in terms of numbers?"

"That's fine, I don't mind sharing," Kevin said. "In the last two years, we've grown significantly—more than doubling, from just under a million to two and a half million. I thought life would be easier and that I would be on easy street by now."

"So, tell everyone what's been happening." I asked.

"What do you mean? I already said I don't have any cash to take home," Kevin replied.

"Has your debt increased?" I asked.

"Um, yeah," Kevin said. "I don't understand it."

"Are you working any less than you did two years ago?" I asked.

"No, I'm actually running harder than ever, even though I've hired an office manager and a project manager," Kevin said.

"Is that all you added in terms of staff?" I asked.

"Well, no, there's the estimator, a safety guy, and I promoted one of our people to field supervisor," Kevin said.

"And what did hiring those people bring you?" I asked.

Blank stare.

"Did your costs go up because of the new hires?" I probed.

"Well, of course, their salaries," Kevin said. "And the payroll taxes that go along with them. Oh, and the workers' comp insurance bill went up. I had to get a bigger office and the rent went up. Plus, I bought desks, computers, software, office supplies, and probably a whole lot more that I can't even think of right now. So I screwed myself up, but how was I supposed to grow?"

"Relax, Kevin," I said. "What you did was a perfectly natural and normal response to growth. Can I keep going with the questions?"

"I'm afraid to say yes, but go ahead," Kevin said.

"Tell me what has happened to your receivables and payables during this time?" I asked.

"I don't follow," Kevin said.

"If your sales have doubled, have your accounts receivable doubled too?" I asked.

"Yes, come to think of it, they at least doubled," Kevin responded. "How did you know?"

"I bet your payables doubled, too, correct? How about overall debt?" I asked.

"Did you somehow get a look at my financial statements?" Kevin asked.

"I didn't have to," I said. "I've seen it time and time again with contractors."

"So how are all of these guys doing better than me?" Kevin asked. He looked miserable.

"I will let them answer that," I said. "Anybody, are you really doing better?"

"It has been a struggle for me too," Paul admitted. "It's starting to get better, but the same was true for me during my company's growth spurt a few years ago."

One by one, each of the contractors chimed in. Some had already experienced challenges with growth, others were going through it now, but all of them admitted that they weren't where they wanted to be.

"I'm glad I'm not alone," Kevin said, relieved. "I guess the old saying about the grass being greener is true, but that doesn't solve my problem. Can I fix it?"

"Believe it or not, you have already started to solve it yourself," I said. "You have put a system into place that helps. And you should know that I have seen many construction companies grow themselves right out of business because of this exact thing."

"Was that what happened with Precision Prime?" Alex asked.

"Could be. From what you guys told me, the signs were there. Cash flow problems and mismanagement of finances are two of the top reasons contractors go out of business."

"So Profit First helps with growth? How?" Kevin asked.

"Let me start by explaining this a bit," I said. "When a construction company grows, it is actually very common for its overhead to grow at a faster rate than its top line."

"Why is that, Wade?" Roger asked.

"You guys demonstrated why just now," I replied. "When you have money coming in, it's easy to spend it. Do you think all of those construction companies that run their business off of one bank account have a better barometer than you do?"

"Maybe they got their job cost software working," Pam joked.

"Maybe, maybe not, but the thing is, they have been looking at profitability from a financial statement perspective. You people are now looking at it through a cash flow lens."

"Still don't follow," Roger said.

"Alex, what will happen if you overspend in your OpEx account?" I asked.

"I will run out of money," Alex replied.

"Right," I said. "If your percentages are dialed in, you are in growth mode, and all of a sudden you find yourself with a cash deficit from out-of-the-ordinary expenses, you might be overextending yourself and you will have to make some decisions."

"What kind of decisions?" Roger asked.

"Decisions like, do you need to cut overhead? What is actually great is that you have built a natural guardrail against overspending into your system and will notice when you borrow from other accounts. If nothing else, you can't actually spend faster than your cash growth rate without making some kind of change." I saw some of the guys nodding.

"Change what?" Roger asked.

"Either you need to find a few more percentage points in your allocation somewhere or you can't swing it," I said. "Which leads to the bigger epiphany."

"Which is?" Alex asked.

"That you have naturally developed some percentages to use when you bid your jobs," I said. "And you now bid for profit, in cash, and not from a financial statement approach. When you can capitalize on that, you'll really start to develop profit in your business."

"Back to my situation. What should I do?" Kevin asked.

"Go back and look at your OpEx allocation percentage," I said. "If it isn't keeping up, you may need to cut some overhead, raise your prices, find more profitable jobs, or use some combination of these approaches. That should give you a starting point."

"I've got my homework, then," Kevin said.

///

CHAPTER 14 END NOTES
Managing Cash Flow in Uncertain Times

WHEN A CONSTRUCTION COMPANY GROWS, it can feel like there's finally extra money to spend. A big retainage check, or extra cash in the bank, can make it tempting to buy new equipment, hand out bonuses, or reward yourself for hard work. But having more money on hand doesn't always mean the company is ahead, and it's easy to overlook future bills and obligations.

The Construction Growth/Profit Paradox happens when growth leads to less cash, not more. While taking on bigger or more jobs seems like it should increase profits, it often brings higher costs related to hiring new staff, renting more office space, or buying additional equipment. These expenses tend to grow faster than revenue, and the company may also take on more debt while waiting for receivables to come in. This creates a cash crunch, in which money flows out faster than it comes in.

To avoid this trap, it is essential to manage cash carefully during growth periods. Which is not about spending what's in the bank now but ensuring that there's enough working capital to fund the business. Using a system to allocate money for reserves, overhead, and future expenses will help keep the business stable even as it expands.

Profit First offers a straightforward system for tackling the Growth/ Profit Paradox by providing structure and consistency in managing cash flow. Allocating income to different accounts for specific needs guards against overspending and ensures that the company has the cash needed for its most critical obligations. By sticking to predetermined percentages, owners avoid the temptation to use surplus funds unwisely, helping to balance the pressures of growth.

During periods of rapid expansion, Profit First encourages companies to reassess their overhead allocation. Growth often brings higher expenses that can outpace revenue. By regularly reviewing and adjusting their overhead percentages, companies can remain aligned with actual cash flow. Additionally, they can increase prices to reflect rising costs or focus on more profitable projects to help stabilize finances. When paired with trimming nonessential overhead, these strategies enable a business to grow without becoming overextended.

The big takeaway is that Profit First shifts the focus from financial statement profitability to cash-based profitability. This means bidding on projects with real cash flow in mind, not just theoretical profits on paper. Using this cash-based perspective, construction companies can better predict their needs, avoid financial shortfalls, and build sustainable profitability even during times of growth. The system provides the discipline and clarity needed to manage the challenges of expansion while maintaining financial stability.

If your company is experiencing growth, follow the guidelines below to avoid growing at a rate that is faster than you can afford, and spot and address trouble before it becomes a crisis.

Guidelines for Managing Growth in a Construction Company

1. **Evaluate Cash Flow Regularly**
   a. Perform a weekly or biweekly review of all account balances.
   b. Reassess allocation percentages so they align with the company's current growth phase.
   c. Use actual cash flow, not just projected revenue, to guide financial decisions.

2. **Stick to the Allocation System**
   a. Allocate every dollar that comes in according to your Profit First percentages and avoid making exceptions for large payments or "windfalls."
   b. **Profit Account**: Secure a portion for long-term sustainability.
   c. **Owner's Compensation Account**: Ensure fair compensation for your role in the company.
   d. **Tax Account**: Set aside taxes to avoid future surprises.
   e. **OpEx (Operating Expenses) Account**: Cover overhead and operating costs responsibly.
   f. **JobEx (Job Expenses) Account**: Ensure that funds are available for project-related costs.

3. **Prioritize Reserves**
   a. Build up reserves to handle fluctuations in cash flow.
   b. Aim for two to four months' worth of operating expenses as a buffer.

    c. Use retainage and extra cash flow to strengthen reserves before making new investments.

4. Address Overhead and Costs

    a. Reassess Overhead: Compare current overhead to income growth and adjust as needed.

    b. Trim Nonessential Costs: Identify and cut unnecessary expenses.

    c. Review Pricing: Ensure that pricing reflects job and operating expense increases.

5. Manage Debt Wisely

    a. Prioritize paying down high-interest debt.

    b. Avoid taking on new debt unless it is absolutely necessary and make sure your goals are aligned with cash flow projections.

    c. Use Profit First allocations to systematically reduce debt without sacrificing other critical needs.

6. Focus on Profitable Projects

    a. Analyze job profitability and prioritize high-margin projects.

    b. Avoid taking on projects with tight margins that could strain cash flow during growth.

7. Plan for Large Purchases

    a. Delay nonessential purchases until reserves are funded and cash flow is stable.

    b. For necessary investments, create a dedicated savings plan in a CapEx account.

    c. Avoid impulsive spending on equipment or bonuses without evaluating future obligations.

8. Monitor Accounts Receivable and Payable

    a. To maintain healthy cash flow, collect accounts receivable promptly.

b. Keep accounts payable under control by paying invoices on time (but not ahead of schedule unless necessary).

9. **Regularly Review Financial Health**

   a. Conduct quarterly reviews of cash flow, Profit First allocations, and overall financial performance.

   b. Identify areas where growth is causing strain and adjust your strategy accordingly.

   c. Use this opportunity to refine percentages and prepare for continued growth.

10. **Stay Disciplined**

    a. Resist the temptation to change allocations for large deposits or perceived windfalls.

    b. Use the Profit First system as a framework to guide decisions, even when growth feels overwhelming.

    c. Rely on the built-in guardrails of the system to maintain stability and avoid financial overextension.

PART 5

FINISHING TOUCHES FOR LASTING FINANCIAL STABILITY

CHAPTER 15
Sustaining Success: Developing Permanent Profitability

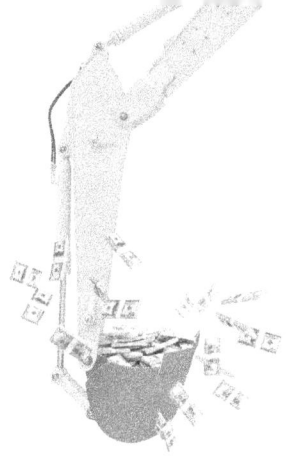

Gaining Confidence with Cash Flow

IT HAD BEEN OVER A month since I met with the crew, and they were ready for next steps. The project was nearing completion, and I was quite impressed with what the group had accomplished, all while learning about and implementing Profit First in their own businesses.

I had advised most of them on their quarterly distributions, and they were now two or three in and starting to get into the rhythm.

The meeting began with the usual barrage of updates and schedule discussions, then transitioned into a conversation about an extended change order issue that seemed to go on forever. Once we got past that, Alex asked me to take over.

I opened with the usual check-in. "Looks like you've been doing great without me," I said. "I'm eager to hear about your progress and if you have had any challenges."

"I'll start us off," Alex said. "Things are great on my end. I've managed to hold onto the cash and make sure everyone gets paid properly as we go. I know what I have to spend. We've made some progress on our job cost system. It's still not perfect, but even without it, I can tell how things are progressing with the bank accounts. Just having control over where the cash is going is huge for me. When things get tight, I can control the cash because I have a better handle on what we have to spend."

The whole RGC crew, including Dan, was here this time and sitting in the front row beside him. I turned to Pam.

"Pam, what are your thoughts?" I asked.

"I know I was skeptical about all the extra bank accounts," Pam said, "but it actually makes things easier for me. There are fewer interruptions, and I don't have to scramble to cut a check just because someone showed up at the door. It makes a lot more sense now."

"It has forced me to make some tough choices," Roger said. "For instance, I saw that we needed to cut overhead, including letting go of a particular truck."

Dan was sitting right by him. I was afraid of what was to come, but asked anyway, "Dan?"

"I admit it," Dan replied, "that truck was a dumb purchase. As much as I wanted to resist your system, I see how controlled this job is. I guess I still have some things to learn."

"Great, thank you, Dan," I said, relieved to get a civil answer. "More quick check-ins, everyone. Elvis, you're next."

"Think I've got it now," Elvis said. "My percentages are dialed in, and I just stick with them. The Colonel sends her regards."

"Nice," I said. "Mark?"

"Well, ditto what Elvis said," Mark replied. "Things have started to smooth out on my end too. It's been a learning curve, but I can see the benefits now, especially when I look at the numbers."

"One more and we'll move on to today's topic," I said. "Kevin, have you got an update on your growth and cash flow?"

"I'm finally starting to see those rewards," Kevin said. "I'm not just paying my crew on time; I'm finally taking a regular paycheck home now. It's been a game changer for keeping things steady on the jobsite and I can see brighter days ahead."

"That's fantastic," I said, "but this is not the time to get complacent for any of you. Hopefully you are past the need to allocate income every single day and are better able to control your rhythm. I also hope you are less tempted to raid your Profit accounts."

The Power of Profit Discipline

"Uh-huh," Elvis said. "I get it now. It was so tempting to dip into the Profit account when cash was tight. Once I forced myself to leave it alone, it started to grow. Seeing that balance build really boosted my confidence. It's making a difference."

"Great," I said. "If we raid profit any time we want, we haven't learned anything. We need to remember to let it accumulate and then take our profit distribution on a quarterly basis. Like a kid waiting for Christmas, the anticipation of taking that profit is exciting. You don't want to be the kid who insists on getting the toy right now because that doesn't teach financial discipline."

"Can we go back through some of those profit distribution rules again?" Alex asked.

"Of course," I said. "That was on the agenda. Then we'll move on to special annual reviews and maintaining the system. I have a few advanced concepts to share with you today."

"I don't know about everybody else," Alex said, "but I'm ready for more."

"Go for it," Paul replied.

Quarterly Profit Distribution: Staying on Track

"OK, FIRST, A QUICK REVIEW of what to do quarterly," I said. "Remember, you need to accumulate your profit on a quarterly basis before distributing it. I usually recommend taking half the profit to reward yourself and retaining the other half to support growth."

"Right," Alex said.

"Also, we talked about the fact that as your company grows, the need for capital grows as well," I said. "If your company doubles, the amount of money you need to sustain it will double too. This is a good time to think about reducing debt, increasing working capital, or setting aside money for a rainy-day fund. Having a few months of overhead in the bank can eliminate a lot of sleepless nights worrying about covering payroll."

"I won't miss that," Alex said.

"If you can accomplish that," I said, "you might find that you can increase your line of credit and bonding capacity, which can further the growth. At the end of each quarter, you should also assess your allocation percentages and see if they are still in line. We've talked about these things before."

"Can we go into more detail with that part?" Alex asked.

"You read my mind," I said.

Annual Review: Planning for the Future

"OVER THE PAST SEVERAL MONTHS," I said, "we've talked about various factors that can impact construction companies. How often did you actually sit down and examine the direction your construction company was heading before you started this journey? Annually? Quarterly?"

"Can I say never?" Roger replied.

"Yeah, it's nice to think about but easy to let slide," Alex said.

"Exactly," I replied. "This can't be a static process. We need to stay on top of changes every quarter and there are some special things we should do at the end of the year. What do you guys think we should focus on during quarterly reviews?"

"We definitely need to check if we've borrowed from one bank account to cover another," Alex said. "That's a red flag, right?"

"Absolutely," I agreed. "If you did that, there was a reason for it. Has revenue increased or decreased? Did seasonality play a part? Was it because of a one-time, unexpected expense, or has something changed?"

"I haven't had to in a while, but with the slowdown I see coming in the winter months, I need to start thinking about when and how much I'm going to need," Mark said thoughtfully.

"Good point, Mark," I said. "Your approach has become proactive, and that's fantastic. Looking further ahead, we've discussed growth and decline cycles of a construction company. What economic factors are you guys seeing in this area or your type of construction?"

"Residential is still going strong," Alex said, "but commercial jobs are starting to dry up."

Preparing for Growth or Decline

"Good observation," I said. "Managing cash flow in construction is all about predicting what's on the horizon as best we can. So, if you've noticed a decline or the potential for one, what should your first move be?"

"Cutting costs," Elvis answered quickly. "But that's easier said than done."

"True, that could be one approach," I said. "You could also look for additional revenue streams or take a whole host of other approaches. What we have to do is evaluate the cash flow impact and strategize what will be necessary to get through it. If a decline seems like it might be more long-term, we may need to make some tougher decisions. Thoughts?"

"What if we see expansion happening instead?" Roger asked. "Maybe it's time to move to a bigger facility if the business is growing, or hire more staff? I guess we need to figure out what that would do to our overhead."

"And cash flow," Alex added.

"Good," I said. "This is exactly where I wanted to go with it. Roger, if you see things expanding, ask yourself if it's because you have taken on more low-margin work. Have you changed your pricing? Are you regularly reviewing costs?"

"Good questions. I know I'm not looking at that as often as I should," Mark chimed in, "but it's on my list."

"These are just some of the things to consider that affect your cash flow," I said. "Reviewing expenditures is crucial, especially when you're trying to improve your profit margins. Take software subscriptions, for example—are they still necessary, or are your needs changing? And if you need to make new purchases due to growth or market changes, now's the time to plan for them. Any big purchases on the horizon?"

"I might need to replace some old equipment," Elvis said, "but I'm holding off for the moment. So can I come out of the asylum now?"

I laughed. "Yes, but remember if your needs change, that may also need to change," I said. "How about personal priorities? Have any of those changed? Anybody see them affecting their cash needs?"

"Yeah," Mark said, "with my kids starting high school, I'm thinking a lot more about college savings. It's not cheap and I need to start putting money aside now."

"Same here," Elvis said, "but for a different reason. Retirement's creeping up on me, and I haven't saved nearly enough."

"I've been dreaming about a quiet spot in the mountains," Roger said, "or maybe by the beach."

"That's exactly the kind of thing you need to be talking and thinking about," I said. "How have your priorities changed? Maybe you want to work less and start training someone to take over."

"That thought has crept into my mind more and more in the last few years," Roger said.

"Roger, that's smart," I said. "We should all be planning for what's next—or considering what happens if we get hit by a beer truck. If stepping back is on your mind, start thinking about what that looks like for you in the next year and beyond."

"That's a lot to think about," Alex said.

"True," I said, "but in essence, I'm telling you to review your allocation percentages on a quarterly basis and adjust as necessary. Also, once a year, take some time to think about what comes next and what it will take to get you where you want to go."

"This has been great. Thank you, Wade," Alex said. "I think we've all learned a lot on this journey."

"Let me know when the job is done," I said.

"Will do!" Alex replied.

//

CHAPTER 15 END NOTES
Ongoing Maintenance for Permanent Profitability

THE KEY MESSAGE IN THIS chapter is that the Profit First system is not static and must always adapt. As we have discussed in previous chapters, construction changes over time. This is evidenced by everything from material cost spikes due to supply chain issues, to economic ups and downs, to factors unique to you and your company. Your situation can change in an instant. Improving technology, making that next great hire, borrowing to buy a new piece of equipment, and a whole host of other things can affect your cash flow.

One key thing that you have hopefully figured out by now is that your Profit First system will keep things in check for you. As I've said, it can be an early warning signal that things have changed.

Changes aside, the primary purpose of the system is to ensure that you, the owner, take home the money you deserve—not only for doing what you do for the company, but also to reward you for taking the risk to be in business. Keep this in mind when you are reviewing your system; it may mean controlling expenses so you can allocate another percentage point or two toward your profitability, owner's compensation, or to pay the taxes on that profit.

You may not be at the end of the quarter or the end of the year as you read this, so no homework is required unless you are at that stage. This chapter should serve as a reference for you to revisit when that time comes.

To that end, here's a quick recap of what you should do on a quarterly basis when it is time to distribute your profit, plus a checklist of some things to consider at least annually. There is no way this checklist could be complete, so you may want to add items to it that apply specifically to you.

Profit First Quarterly Steps (Quick Recap)

1. **Profit Distribution**: Accumulate your profit until the quarter's end in your Profit account. At that point, consider allocating 50% to the owner as a personal reward and retaining the remaining 50% for business growth. If you are deep in debt, you may want to use some profit to pay off debt; adapt allocations to your situation as necessary.

2. **Review Allocation Percentages**: Evaluate whether your percentages still align with your company's current financial position and goals. Adjust them with an eye toward finding additional percentages from JobEx or OpEx for Residual Revenue to allocate to your Profit, Owner's Compensation, or Tax accounts.

3. **Cash Flow Assessment**: Review whether cash was borrowed between accounts and investigate the root causes. Identify any seasonal trends or unexpected expenses that may be impacting your cash flow.

4. **Strategic Adjustments**: Address any short-term needs like expected shortfalls and ensure that adequate reserves are available. Reassess upcoming projects or changes that may require adjustment to your spending or savings.

Profit First Annual Review Checklist

1. **Financial Performance Review**

   a. **Revenue Trends**

   - Analyze revenue growth or decline over the past year.
   - Identify key drivers (e.g., market conditions, seasonality, and project types).

   b. **Profitability Analysis**

   - Review profit margins across projects.
   - Ensure that pricing aligns with desired profitability targets.

2. **Cash Flow Management**

   a. **Account Borrowing**: Check to see whether special transfers occurred between accounts and why.

   b. **Seasonality and Trends**: Assess historical cash flow patterns to forecast the upcoming year.

   c. **Working Capital**: Ensure that reserves are sufficient for operational needs (e.g., payroll and overhead).

3. **Overhead and Expenditures Audit**

   a. **Cost Cutting**: Eliminate unnecessary and underutilized expenses (e.g., subscriptions and equipment).

   b. **Efficiency Improvements**: Evaluate cost efficiency of systems and processes.

   c. **Overhead Impact**: Assess how changes to overhead affect cash flow and profitability.

4. **Growth and Expansion Planning**

   a. **Market Analysis**: Evaluate potential growth areas and declining market sectors.

   b. **Facility and Staffing Needs**: Plan for potential expansion (e.g., new hires, larger facilities).

c. **Strategic Investments**: Budget for major purchases (e.g., equipment and software).

5. **Equipment and Asset Management**

   a. **Replacement Planning**: Identify aging or underperforming equipment that needs replacement.

   b. **Growth Adjustments**: Plan for additional resources needed to scale operations.

6. **Personal and Business Goals Alignment**

   a. **Personal Priorities**: Reflect on life changes (e.g., the need to save for retirement or college tuition) and their impact on cash flow.

   b. **Succession Planning**: Examine whether you need to begin transitioning leadership or planning for reduced involvement.

   c. **Financial Security**: Ensure that the business supports your long-term personal financial goals.

7. **Strategic Forecasting**

   a. **Economic Factors**: Analyze local and industry-wide economic trends.

   b. **Proactive Adjustments**: Prepare for anticipated downturns or growth with tailored strategies.

   c. **Scenario Planning**: Develop contingency plans for both positive and negative shifts in business conditions.

CHAPTER 16

A New Dawn: Reclaiming Control and Purpose

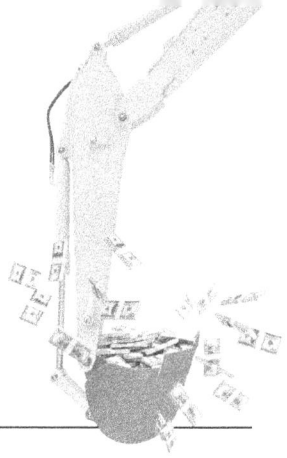

A Call from Roger

It had been about six weeks since I last met with the crew. I knew they were in the final stages of the school job, tackling the punch list items and getting ready to turn the project over to the school board. The group had been keeping in touch with me through email. I knew they were getting tired, but also that there was a real sense of satisfaction in the air; they could see the finish line.

Then, on a rainy Tuesday morning, a call came into my office with a message to call Roger back as soon as possible. He had never called my office directly before; it was always Alex or Pam who reached out. As I walked back to my office to make the call, I stared at the little yellow sticky note and wondered what had happened.

My mind raced as I sat on hold waiting for Pam to transfer my call.

"Hi, Wade," Roger said. He sounded cheerful; I exhaled in relief. "Can you do me a big favor?" he asked.

"Sure, I can try," I said nervously, not knowing what I was about to agree to.

"Could you help me set up a surprise lunch for Alex on the eighteenth to celebrate the successful completion of the project?" Roger asked.

"Glad to do it," I said, even more relieved. "Can I pick the place?"

"Megan's?" Roger asked.

"That's what I was thinking," I said.

"Great minds think alike," Roger said. "Could you put me in touch with her?"

"Sure thing. I'll email you her phone number," I said.

After Roger emailed me to confirm that he had arranged the lunch with Megan, I called Alex and asked if he would like to meet me for lunch the following Friday. He was eager to let me know how things had been going and gladly agreed.

That day, I arrived a bit early to wait for Alex in the parking lot. When he pulled in, I waved him over. "Ready for lunch?"

"Absolutely," Alex replied with a smile. "But what happened? There are hardly any cars in the parking lot. Are they closed?"

"Trust me, they're open," I said.

We walked through the thick glass doors to see Megan standing there with a huge grin on her face, the kind of smile I remembered from when she originally opened her restaurant. I hadn't seen her in many months, and the dark circles under her eyes were gone. She looked happier than I had ever seen her.

Restaurants aren't my specialty, so I had shared some Profit First insights with her and then introduced her to another trusted Mastery-Certified Profit First Professional who specialized in adapting the system for restaurants. My friend had told me in passing that Megan had completely transformed her business, but I hadn't gotten the details. I could see now what they meant without looking at the books. It was quite apparent that things had improved. The bar was completely full, and she had replaced her secondhand fixtures with new models.

A Surprise Celebration

"WHERE ARE ALL OF THE customers?" Alex asked.

"I've still got them, not to worry. Come with me," Megan said as she waved us around the register.

As we walked around the corner, Alex's face lit up. All the subcontractors from the high school job had gathered to celebrate, and standing in the middle of the room was Alex's wife, Helen, beaming proudly. She greeted Alex with a long kiss before he could say a word.

"Helen! What are you doing here?" Alex asked.

Roger stepped up beside her, grinning. "I invited her. We thought it was time for some extra support for a special announcement."

Alex looked around in shock and amazement. "You guys did all this?"

"We all just want to say thank you, Alex," Roger said. "You saw the cash flow problems early on, before they got worse for us. I see now that they could easily have put us under. You had the foresight to bring in help to implement a cash flow system that literally saved our business. The job is done, and we all wanted to celebrate the success you've brought us."

Acknowledging the Transformation

ALEX LOOKED AROUND, TAKING IT all in. "You guys did the work. I just made sure we stayed on track."

Elvis walked up and handed Alex a bottle of his favorite beer. "You did more than that. For the first time, I feel in control of our equipment budget. Repairs used to feel like emergencies every time. Now, I've got funds ready for breakdowns. It's like being ready for rain with a good umbrella," he laughed. "Instead of scrambling, we're ready for repairs before they happen."

Pam joined in the conversation. "I thought that keeping up with all the accounts would be a lot of work," she said with a smile. "But planning and getting a rhythm for payments has made life so much easier. No more rushing to pay everyone as soon as a check arrives. Now it feels like I'm running the books, not the other way around."

"Let's grab some food, everyone," Roger said. He handed Alex and Helen plates and insisted that they go first. As they walked toward the bar, I pulled Pam aside to ask the obvious question. "I notice the whole company is here except Dan. Where is he?"

"Um, not my place to say since it isn't common knowledge," she said. "I'm sure you will hear about it soon enough."

"OK," I said, puzzled but thinking I had better not press. We got in line behind all the hungry subcontractors and heaped our plates with Megan's fresh, delicious food. As we all sat down together around the tables that had been pushed together to form one long gathering place, I relished the laughter and banter among the crowd. They had truly come a long way.

As people began to finish their main course and start toward the dessert bar, Peter, usually the quiet one, stood up and said, "Before we get dessert, I want to say thanks to Alex, Roger, and RGC for including me on this job. For years, I was just going in circles with debt. Every time I thought I was making headway, something pulled me back. Now, I've got a plan. My debt is steadily going down, month by month. I'm not just hanging on—I'm moving forward."

Paul, who was sitting next to Peter, stood next. "I want to second that. Setting real profit goals was a game changer for me. I used to think profit was just something on paper. I had never seen it in my bank account," he said with a laugh. "Now I set goals and see that cash coming in. I haven't missed a paycheck since we got our first draw on this job. It's not just numbers—it's real to me now. Thank you, Alex!"

At that point, three other people jumped up and started speaking at the same time. After some laughter, Jake remained standing to say, "Controlling job costs used to feel like chasing my own tail. I didn't have any system; I just crossed my fingers. Now, I've got a handle on it. It's not perfect, but I know where the money's going, and I can adjust before things get out of hand."

Kevin was next, saying, "I never really understood our overhead—at least, not in a practical way. For the first time, I have a system to track it and cash I can count on. It's helped me bid jobs right. I've got a whole new perspective."

Next up was Mark. "Let's raise a glass. Alex, a toast to you!" Everyone clinked glasses. "With concrete, there's always a slow season," Mark went on. "We used to just hope we'd make it through. Now, I've got cash set aside for the slow months. No more stressing come winter— we've got a cushion, and I know I can survive."

The Next Chapter for RGC

Then Roger stood and said, "I've got an announcement before everyone leaves. As some of you may have noticed, Dan is not here. He has decided that he wants to try and become a pilot, so I have sent him to flight school to allow him to explore that on his own. He's my son, and I always thought he would be the one to take over my business. To be sure, Dan has learned some valuable lessons, but I've also come to realize that he is not the right fit and unqualified to take over. Alex, I'm promoting you to Chief Operations Officer."

I watched Alex's expression turn to one of surprised shock. Clearly humbled by the unexpected promotion, he simply nodded in quiet acceptance, processing the weight of this new responsibility.

Helen, who had been anxiously following the company's ups and downs, gave him a huge, proud smile.

Roger continued, "I haven't told you this before, but I want you to succeed me in the business. You are the future of this company, and I believe you can build it into something even greater."

Alex, not usually at a loss for words, stood and started in a cracked voice, "Thank you all. Thank you for your hard work. It took everyone to pull this off.

"I learned a lot in this restaurant about cash flow," he continued. "Accumulating income in one place, allocating it to different accounts for specific purposes in a particular order, keeping a consistent rhythm, and learning to control temptation. I guess we've all come a long way from chasing down checks on Thursday to cover payroll on Friday."

After a few comments from around the room, Alex said, "With all of the growth in town, I heard the county is looking to build another new high school. They're taking bids in a few months. Anybody game?"

The excited response was unanimous.

People started to file out of the restaurant, hugging Alex or patting him on the back on their way. I was standing nearby when Alex asked Roger if he was needed back at the office right away.

"No, but I need to talk to you about some things. Where are you going?" Roger asked.

"Got to go see some people about the job," Alex replied as he kissed Helen and said his goodbyes to those who were still there. He walked to his truck, jumped in, and took off.

Alex told me later where he went that afternoon after lunch and why. At first, he didn't know where he was going; he just needed to drive. But after a few minutes, he found himself at the shiny new school they had built. It would open soon.

A Moment of Reflection

ALEX PULLED INTO THE FRESHLY paved parking lot with its bright white striping that had just been completed the day before, stopped in front of the main entrance, and gazed at the new bright doors that were painted with the new school colors, navy blue and gold. Memories of his own high school days came flooding back. Thousands of young adults would walk through these doors to make their own memories in the coming decades.

After taking one last look at his handiwork, he decided to jump on the interstate and just drive without a destination. He headed east. After ten minutes, he knew where he needed to go. As he pulled off the exit ramp to his old neighborhood, he drove by his old high school.

Alex hadn't been back here since the day of the bid opening. As he drove slowly toward the entrance, he noticed a beautiful new sign where the old "Shoo" sign had been. It was a community center now, and there were several cars in the parking lot. He looked at the freshly painted, bright white trim. The old bones of this building had a new purpose now.

He headed up to his spot where he had parked under the tree. Pulling in, he could already see down into the valley, and the building where he had worked his first high school job. The dingy blue building with broken windows of two years before had been freshly painted cream, with bright red trim, and had brand-new windows. He could see a full parking lot with people buzzing about and a forklift unloading lumber and roof trusses from a truck.

As he sat under the shade tree, Alex thought about what had brought him to this spot on that fateful day. He wondered if there was some kid down there starting his first job, learning to love a new craft and marveling at what he was creating—finding that pride in showing off his newfound knowledge and what he had built with his hands.

At that moment, Alex realized he had found that joy for himself again. He was proud of what he had accomplished while overcoming all of the odds that had seemed to be stacked against him in the construction world. He no longer borrowed from the next job to pay for the last. Like his old high school, his foundation had stood solid, but now the soul was back.

Alex's phone rang. He knew from the ringtone that it was Helen. As he glanced at the phone, he realized that he had left Megan's two hours before.

"Hey, everything OK?" Alex answered.

"Yeah, just wondering when you were coming home. I thought we could go out and celebrate," Helen replied.

"I would love that," Alex replied, "especially since Roger handed me a huge bonus check on the way out the door from lunch. The way we're set up now, I can focus on spending more time with you and the kids. Let me make a call to the office and I will head home."

"I'll be ready," Helen replied. "Love you!"

"Love you too," Alex said.

He hung up and immediately dialed Pam's cell phone.

"Hey Pam, is Roger looking for me?" Alex asked.

"Hey. No. He had a message for you, though," Pam replied.

"Uh-oh, what's that?" Alex asked.

"He said to have a great weekend and that he's excited to talk on Monday," Pam replied.

"I'm looking forward to Monday too. We not only have projects to build, but a business to build as well," Alex said with excitement.

"Can't wait!" Pam said.

"I've just got to make one call early tomorrow morning," Alex said.

///

CHAPTER 16 END NOTES
A New Dawn

THANK YOU FOR READING THIS far. It means a lot to me that you've taken the time to invest in yourself and your business. Writing this book was a labor of love, driven by my desire to share these principles with contractors like you. My goal has always been to help more people than I could ever reach one on one, and it's been an honor to guide you through this journey.

This mission started years ago in the aftermath of the 2008 recession, when I saw too many hardworking contractors lose everything. It was heartbreaking, and it sparked my determination to find a way to help others avoid the same fate. Since then, I've applied these principles in my own firm, and I'm proud to say that they've not only brought stability to my business, but also to the countless contractors I've been privileged to work with. The journey hasn't always been easy, but seeing others succeed has made every challenge worthwhile.

I wrote this book because I believe in you. Contractors work harder than anyone else I know, and yet too often, they struggle just to stay afloat. My hope is that what I've shared here will give you the tools to take control of your cash flow, create a stronger future, and finally take home what you deserve for all your hard work.

As you finish this book, take a moment to reflect on your progress—not just what you've read, but all the steps you've already taken toward transforming your business. Change is never easy, but it's worth every ounce of effort. You've shown the courage to confront financial realities and embrace a new way of thinking. That alone is a victory worth celebrating. My hope is that this journey has given you not just the tools to improve your business, but also the confidence to create a better future for yourself and those who depend on you.

Now it's time to take action. Setting up your accounts and doing the regular allocations, even if you are starting with 1% in your profit bucket—every step forward matters. Change doesn't happen overnight, but with consistency and discipline, small steps lead to big results. Imagine a life where you no longer worry about cash flow, where you take home the income you deserve, and where your business provides the stability and security you've worked so hard to achieve. That future is possible, and it starts with the actions you take today.

Finally, I want to encourage you to think about the legacy you're building. The principles you've learned here have the power to not only transform your business but also to impact your employees, your family, and your community. What will your legacy be? How will you take what you've learned and create something that lasts beyond you? My heartfelt wish is for your success—not just in numbers, but in the fulfillment of building a life and business that reflect your hard work, your values, and your dreams.

You've come this far; now go out and create the future you deserve.

ACKNOWLEDGMENTS

WRITING THIS BOOK HAS BEEN a journey—one I could not have taken alone.

First and foremost, I want to thank my wife, Cassie. For over forty years, she has stood by my side, believing in me through every challenge and success. Her unwavering support and patience mean more to me than words can express.

To my entire team at Carpenter & Company, CPAs, and especially Lisa Murray, Amanda Denton, Josh Menzel, Lauren Webb, Lorie Palmer, and Jennifer Fulton: Thank you for allowing me to test ideas, challenge norms, and refine the approaches in this book with you. Your feedback, patience, and willingness to endure multiple iterations of this text have been invaluable.

A special thank you to my marketing team, especially Amanda Darr: Without your guidance, expertise, and relentless encouragement, this book would still be an idea floating around in my head. Your ability to take my ideas and make them accessible to the world has been nothing short of incredible.

AJ Harper and Laura Stone, thank you for helping me understand that writing a book isn't just about getting words on a page; it's about crafting something that truly serves the reader. Your wisdom and support made all the difference in bringing this book to life.

Mike Michalowicz and the entire team at Profit First Professionals: Thank you. Your support and encouragement have been instrumental in making this book a reality. Mike, I'm especially grateful to you for creating a system that has transformed not only my business, but countless others too. Thank you for changing the cash flow game and allowing me to expand on your concepts here, and for all the inspiration and guidance you have provided over the years that I have been privileged to know you.

By the same token, I owe special thanks to Shawn Van Dyke, author of *Profit First for Contractors*, for allowing me to step into his space and publish my version for contractors when he had no obligation to do so. It is truly appreciated.

Finally, to every contractor out there who has struggled with cash flow, questioned whether they'd ever get ahead, or been the last one to get paid—thank you for being my reason to write this book. My hope is that it helps you take control, build stability, and create the business (and life) you deserve.

GLOSSARY OF KEY TERMS

CapEx (Capital Expenditures): In the context of this book, CapEx refers to an **optional bank account** set aside for **major equipment purchases, repairs, and long-term investments** in a construction business. Unlike JobEx, which covers immediate job-related expenses, CapEx is used for **big-ticket items like machinery, vehicles, and major repairs** that impact cash flow over time. The funds for this account must come from **OpEx**, not from JobEx or other allocations. While not every contractor needs a CapEx account, those with significant equipment expenses may benefit from setting aside a portion of OpEx to ensure that they have cash available for planned purchases and unexpected repairs without disrupting their financial system.

CAPs (Current Allocation Percentages): The actual percentage of revenue currently allocated to each financial category in the business, including **JobEx, OpEx, profit, owner's compensation, and tax.** CAPs provide a snapshot of where the company's cash flow is going today, often revealing inefficiencies or imbalances that need adjustment. These percentages are used as a baseline for improving cash flow management.

Cash Commitment Base: The total of **JobEx plus OpEx**, representing the percentage of revenue already committed to covering job costs and operating expenses. **Subtracting this figure from total revenue determines Residual Revenue.** In practical terms, if, for instance, the **Cash Commitment Base** accounts for 88% of total revenue, that leaves only 12% as **Residual Revenue**—the portion available for profit, owner's pay, and taxes. This means that increasing revenue alone won't significantly improve take-home cash unless pricing, expenses, or efficiency are adjusted. The key takeaway is that **working harder won't increase profit unless you also optimize your cost structure and pricing strategy.**

Construction Growth/Profit Paradox: The false expectation that **growth will automatically lead to profit in construction.** Many contractors assume that increasing revenue will result in more cash in their pockets, but in reality, **growth often leads to higher overhead, increased debt, and cash flow struggles.** As companies expand, overhead costs—including payroll, office expenses, and equipment—tend to grow at a faster rate than revenue. If not managed carefully, **rapid or uncontrolled growth can actually push a company deeper into financial stress and even bankruptcy.** This paradox highlights the importance of **cash flow management over chasing top-line revenue growth.**

Drip Account: A **cash reserve system** used to smooth out cash flow fluctuations. Drip accounts are typically used for **seasonality planning, payroll reserves, or equipment savings**—holding money in a separate account and "dripping" it into the operating account as needed. This prevents financial surprises and ensures that funds are available when necessary.

Instant Assessment: A financial exercise from *Profit First* by **Mike Michalowicz**, originally a seventeen-step process designed to compare **Current Allocation Percentages (CAPs) to Target Allocation Percentages (TAPs)** and identify cash flow imbalances. In this book, the process has been reengineered for contractors to focus first on understanding **where their cash is actually going**—particularly to **JobEx and OpEx**—before worrying about setting long-term targets. This simplified approach helps contractors take immediate action without getting overwhelmed.

Job Cost: The total accumulation of all costs directly assigned to a specific job or project. This includes materials, labor, subcontractors, equipment, payroll taxes, workers' compensation insurance, fuel, and other job-related expenses. **Job cost reflects the actual costs incurred to complete a project.**

Job Costing: The **process** of tracking, allocating, and managing job costs to determine the true cost of a project. Job costing ensures that all expenses related to a specific job are captured accurately, allowing contractors to assess profitability and make data-driven decisions.

JobEx (**Job Expenses Account**): A **dedicated bank account** used to pay for all job-related expenses, including materials, labor, subcontractors, equipment rented specifically for the job, and other direct job expenditures, such as bonds. **JobEx is a real-time cash flow tool** that helps contractors separate job-related spending from other business expenses, ensuring that funds are properly allocated and available when needed.

OpEx (**Operating Expenses Account**): A **dedicated bank account** used to cover the general overhead costs of running a construction business that **are not tied to specific jobs**. This includes rent, office payroll, software, insurance, marketing, and other recurring expenses. This account must also cover payments such as payments on debt that are not reflected on the Profit and Loss statement. OpEx **serves as a surrogate measure for overhead**, helping contractors track and manage their cash flow more effectively.

Owner's Compensation: The money allocated to **compensate the owner(s)** for their work in the business. This is separate from profit—it is a separate account set up for covering the role the owner plays in running the company. The **Owner's Compensation account** ensures that owners can take a consistent salary rather than just scraping by on whatever is left at the end of the month.

Overhead: The total cost of running a construction business that is **not directly tied to a specific project**, including expenses like office payroll, rent, insurance, software, marketing, and other general business costs. Traditional overhead analysis takes a **financial statement approach**, but in this book, we use a **cash flow approach** that includes all **actual cash outflows**, even those not reflected on a profit and loss statement. This ensures that contractors fully account for the cash required to sustain their business. Overhead expenses are covered through the **Operating Expenses (OpEx) account** unless further divided into smaller accounts for better cash management.

POT (**Profit, Owner's Compensation, and Tax**): An acronym for the portion of revenue left over after covering **JobEx and OpEx**, representing the same concept as **Residual Revenue**. The **POT is the real cash available for the business owner's profit, owner's compensation, and taxes.** Think of it like a pot of chili—after paying for all job expenses and overhead, whatever remains in the pot is what the owner gets to keep. If there's not much left, the business isn't truly profitable. The key to increasing **POT** isn't just working harder—it's **controlling costs, pricing correctly, and managing cash flow strategically.**

Profit: In the **Profit First System, profit refers to the cash that remains in your bank account at the end of a period after all job and operating expenses have been covered.** Unlike traditional accounting, where profit is often just a number on a financial statement, **Profit First defines profit as an actual increase in your bank account balance.** By consistently setting aside a percentage of revenue into a dedicated **Profit account**, contractors ensure that profit is realized in real cash, reinforcing financial stability and long-term business success.

Real Revenue: A financial metric that removes **pass-through expenses** (such as materials, subcontractor costs, and other direct job expenses) from total revenue. Real Revenue represents the portion of income available to cover overhead, owner's pay, profit, and taxes. **It is the foundation for setting Profit First allocation percentages.**

Residual Revenue: The money left after **JobEx and OpEx** have been accounted for. This is the **true** cash available for owner's compensation, taxes, and profit. Traditional accounting methods often overstate profitability because they ignore cash flow realities—Residual Revenue provides a more accurate measure of what's actually left over.

TAPs (Target Allocation Percentages): The **ideal** percentages of revenue that should be allocated to the **JobEx, OpEx, Profit, Owner's Compensation, and Tax accounts** in a financially healthy business model. TAPs serve as a goal for contractors to gradually shift toward to ensure that they operate profitably while maintaining sustainable expenses. The goal of **Profit First** is to move from CAPs (where you are today) to TAPs (where you need to be) over time.

ABOUT THE AUTHOR

Wade Carpenter, CPA, CGMA, is a Mastery-Certified Profit First Professional and the founder of Carpenter & Company, Cpas, PC, a firm that exclusively serves construction contractors. With over thirty-five years of experience in construction accounting and finance, Wade has dedicated his career to helping contractors master cash flow, increase profitability, and build financially resilient businesses.

Wade's journey into construction accounting and finance began in his early teens, helping his father, a CPA for a midsized sheet metal contractor, with handwritten spreadsheets on green bar paper. After earning his degree in accounting, Wade specialized in accounting, auditing, and taxation for construction contractors at some of the most respected accounting firms—with some of the highest concentrations of construction clients—in Atlanta and the surrounding region. During this time, he gained expertise in job costing, financial management, and cash flow projections. In 1999, he launched his own firm, and then gradually shifted his focus entirely to construction clients. By 2008, 80% of his firm's revenue came from the construction industry—just in time for the financial crisis that devastated many of his clients. That experience deepened his understanding of cash flow survival in construction, shaping the work he does today.

Though initially skeptical of Profit First, Wade reread the book while working with a client and realized the system's potential for construction contractors. After implementing it in his own firm, he saw a financial turnaround and never missed another paycheck. He then joined Profit

First Professionals and became Mastery-Certified, refining the system specifically for contractors. His passion for helping construction business owners take control of their cash flow led him to write *Profit First for Commercial Construction.*

Wade offers **keynotes, webinars, and workshops** for contractors who struggle with cash flow, helping them gain control over their finances, ensure that their payroll is covered, and build profitable businesses.

To inquire about speaking engagements or bulk book orders,
visit **ProfitFirstConstruction.com**
or email **Wade@ProfitFirstConstruction.com.**